HEINEMANN
ENGLISH

David Kitchen   **Mike Hamlin**

HEINEMANN
EDUCATIONAL

Heinemann Educational,
a division of Heinemann Educational Books Ltd,
Halley Court,
Jordan Hill,
Oxford OX2 8EJ.

OXFORD   LONDON   EDINBURGH   MADRID
ATHENS   BOLOGNA   PARIS   MELBOURNE
SIDNEY   AUCKLAND   SINGAPORE   TOKYO
IBADAN   NAIROBI   HARARE   GABARONE
PORTSMOUTH NH(USA)

© David Kitchen, Mike Hamlin 1992

The moral rights of the authors have been asserted.

First published 1992.

Cataloguing in publication data for this title is available from the British Library.

ISBN 0 435 10306 7

Cover photograph courtesy of The Image Bank

Designed by Plum Design, Southampton.

Illustrations by Shirley Bellwood, Michael Charlton Robert Geary, Donald Harley, Marl Peppé, Trevor Ridley and Shirley Tourret.

Printed and bound in Great Britain by Scotprint Ltd, Edinburgh

Acknowledgements

The authors and publishers would like to thank the following for permission to reproduce copyright material.

Amnesty International for extracts from Amnesty International publications; BBC Radio 4 for extracts from *The Archers* 3/6/91 written by Paul Burns; Channel Four Television for extracts from *Autism* produced by Poseidon Films for Channel 4; Tony Curtis for 'Strongman', © Tony Curtis from *Selected Poems 1970-1985*, Poetry Wales Press, 1986; *The Daily Mirror* for 'Courts Will Sting the Rich' 16/1/90 and for front page 5/9/91; Judy Daish Associates for recording of *Request Stop* by Harold Pinter on cassette; Hunt Emerson for 'The Kid Next Door' from *The Comic Book of First Love*, ed. Philip Boys and Corinne Pearlman, Virago Upstarts 1988; The Department of Energy for Powergen/National Power advert; Faber and Faber Ltd for *Request Stop* by Harold Pinter; Fontana for 'Couch Potatoes' by Patricia Marks Greenfield from *Mind and Media*, Fontana 1984; The Guardian for 'Reasearch the Critics Overlook' by Barrie Gunter, 15/4/91; Victor Gollancz Ltd for 'The Eyes Have it' from *Make Your Move* by James Watson, Victor Gollancz Ltd and for extract from *A Handful of Stars* by Rafik Schami, Victor Gollancz Ltd and for 'Mountains of Waste' from *The Young Green Consumer Guide* by John Elkington and Julia Hales, Victor Gollancz 1990; Rex Harley for 'The Man in the Lift' by Rex Harley; *The Independent* for front page 5/9/91 and for 'Screened Off' by Christiana Hardyment 8/7/89; Michael Joseph Ltd for the cover of *Darwin* by Adrian Desmond and James Moore; James Kirkup for 'High Street Smells' by James Kircup; *The Mail on Sunday* for 'Tormented Chimps are free at Last'; The National Autistic Society for 'What is Autism?'; Nottingham Evening Post for 'A Clean Sweep', April 1991; The Office of Population Censuses and Surveys for the Census Advert; *The Observer Magazine* for 'A Day in the Life of a Farmer' 13/8/78; Oxford University Press for extract from *Mary, After the Queen: Memories of a Working Girl* ed. Angel Hewins, © Angela Hewins 1985 and for 'The Telephone Call' from *The Incident Book* by Fleur Adcock 1986;; Peterloo Press for 'It's Mother, You See' from *Furnished Rooms* by Elma Mitchell, Peterloo Poets 1983; Polygon for 'Men Talk' by Liz Lockhead from *True Confessions and New Cliches*; Premier Teas for Typhoo tea advert; Random Century Group for the cover of *Body and Soul* by Anita Roddick and for 'Meet the McKenzies' from *All Right for Some* by Jane L Thomson, Hutchinson 1986; Michael Robinson for 'The Double Benefit When Criminals meet Victims' from *The Listener* 20/2/86; Scholastic Publications Ltd for extracts and cover from *In Reply to Your Advertisement* by John Kirkbride, Andre Deutsch 1988; Searle Consumer Products for advert for Actomite; Martin Secker & Warburg for 'Marcovaldo at the Supermarket' by Italo Calvino; Sepia and Jefrey Elliot for Conversations with Maya Angelou'; Sinclair-Stevenson Ltd for the cover of *Pepys* by Richard Ollard; Hilary Shipman Ltd for 'Television is Good for Your Kids' , Hilary Shipman Ltd, 1989; *The Times Educational Supplement* for '906 Questioned, One Found innocent' by Anne Susskind, TES 30/10/87; Thames Television for extracts from *The Story of An Hour*; *Today* newspaper for front page 9/5/91; Topic Records Ltd and MCPS for recording of 'The Springhill Mine Disaster by Martin Carthy on cassette; Viking for the cover of *A Moment of War* by Laurie Lee; Virago Press for extract from *The Scarlet Thread* by Rachel Barton.

We would also like to thank the following for permission to reproduce photographs on the pages noted.

BBC Television p 103; J Allan Cash pp 77 top left, bottom right, 78, 80 top right, 140 top, middle, 159 bottom; Ecoscene/Hawkes p 119; Mary Evans Picture Library p 106; Christina Gascoigne p 32; Sally & Richard Greenhill pp 80 top left, 140 bottom; Robert Harding Picture library p 77 top right; Angela Hewins p 38; Magnum/J Natchway pp 180, 182, Magnum/L Freed p 181, Magnum/B Barbey p 183; MGM/PATHE & United International Pictures p 136; City of Newcastle upon Tyne p 128 bottom; Oxford & County newspapers p 105; Philip Parkhouse pp 58, 67, 69, 128 top, 129 top, 130, 173, 174; Popperfoto p 105; Rex Features p 137; Chris Ridgers pp 67 top, 75, 108, 120, 124, 129 middle & botom, 131, 132, 150 bottom, 163, 179, 184, 185, 186, 187; Rafik Schami p 31; Topham Picture Source p 139; Virago p 169, 170.

Introduction

Heinemann English book 4 gives you a whole range of stimulating material for use in GCSE courses, including complete short stories, poems, TV and radio scripts, newspaper and magazine articles and a whole range of material for use in discussion and discursive writing.

The **Teachers' Pack** for book 4 provides up-to-date information about GCSE together with photocopiable practice material that can be used with the book in preparing specifically for assessment. It also has a range of further activities and support materials together with clear grids showing the National Curriculum coverage for each unit.

To help you tackle the main types of writing required at GCSE, the reference section at the end of the book has guidelines on creative writing and writing to inform or persuade. There is also a useful section on wider reading with information on books and authors to help you choose what to read either for pleasure or for GCSE.

A brief index right at the back of the book shows where you can find subjects, terms and skills dealt with in the units. There are also photocopiable reference sheets on a large range of skills and techniques in the **Heinemann English Assessment and Reference File**.

There is also a cassette with recordings linked to the units in the book. Material on cassette is indicated in the book by a symbol like the one opposite. A full list of the cassette's contents is also given opposite.

We hope you find **Heinemann English** challenging, thought provoking, useful, and, above all, enjoyable.

Cassette Contents

Contents

Words for their own sake: reading and writing literature

Words to communicate

STRANGER
THAN FICTION

As you are reading this story by James Watson, think about how you would like it to finish and how it might actually finish.

The little girl who has come up the steps of the double-decker stares at Gina. It is a stare of such penetrating hatred that, for a moment, Gina holds her gaze as if doing so might reveal some mistake. But the girl's stare is for her. Its withering concentration is for her.

The child kneels on the seat in front of Gina, and facing her. She presses herself against the backrest, gripping the chrome frame with tight fingers.

Do I know you, and yet have somehow forgotten? Gina cannot remember ever seeing this child before. The face is oval and pale. It is sharp, stretched; harshly pretty. Her eyes burn. I hate you. I detest you. There is no doubt about their message.

You are sixteen, Gina reminds herself. This child is eight, maybe nine. This is a game. Sensible sixteen year olds know better than to play games with strangers, even this young.

You've got to be careful what you do with your eyes. So the book said. Not this book in Gina's hands, page half read, but the book on how you say things – say so much – without speaking; without words.

It's a tease. Look away.

Gina resumes her reading. She is disturbed. She feels the gaze of the child, its hostility, ramming at her lowered eyelids, piercing them. Read.

Concentrate. This could be good practice. The story is about a soldier returning from war. His face has been burnt away by an incendiary bomb. He is unrecognisable. He enters a Scottish seaport as dusk falls. His lover lives at the end cottage overlooking the harbour wall.

Gina reassures herself. It is the story which is making you tense, not this child. You are anticipating how the soldier's beautiful girl will respond as she looks upon her faceless lover. It is a test. Yes, for the reader as well as the girl.

Turning the page, Gina looks up and meets once more the face of the child – staring, staring. Right at you, right into you. It is on the tip of her tongue to say, "Do you mind not staring?" Should I break the ice, crack a joke and crack the stare? No. Silence is best. Little girls ought not to talk to strangers, even to bigger girls who feel intimidated by them.

No one is safe these days. Dad said. Mum says, Absolutely no one. Whatever happened to kindness? And remember the eyes.

It seems to be the end of the incident, for the girl's mother, who has been paying the fares below, comes up from the lower deck. Same hard face, but thankfully eyes that are not staring. She wears a heavy full-length coat despite the summer heat. Worn, thinks Gina. A worn-out person. Her handbag is not properly closed.

"There," she says, dropping down on to the seat beside her daughter. It is almost amusing, for she bounces down, as if she too enjoys a game. "All set, eh?"

The child turns on one knee, reluctant to surrender her incursion into Gina's private space. She leans towards her mother as if to touch heads. Gina is about to read again, but holds off a moment as the child immediately raises her hand as a barricade and begins to whisper in her mother's ear. She does so brazenly, all the while staring – staring and staring – at Gina.

Whispering. Long and feverishly. About me.

She ponders, How can you be so afraid? – of a mere child, on a bus in the middle of a sunlit day. Don't be stupid. Read. The faceless soldier has reached the end-terrace house. Rain sweeps in from the sea. Cold, stabbing rain. It runs across the scars where his eyebrows had been.

A gas lamp at the street corner betrays without mercy his red injuries.

It is the wrong time to come. It is the witching hour; but the stubbornness within him will have it no other way. He has borne his injury too long alone.

"Well if she does that again, there'll be trouble." The mother's voice is no whisper. She has turned her head only a fraction, but the words have been unmistakenly cast behind her at Gina; in a tone of warning.

And the message continues. The words pour into the receptive ear. "Is that so? Is that so then?" Now a glance around. "Oh." A stare: the burning stare. "Is that so?" Quite aloud. Don't the others on the bus hear? "She did? Well just this once more, believe me."

Gina shifts her own gaze as if it were something heavy, which suddenly needed manoeuvring like furniture. Lifting it, heaving it from the page; angling it away from the nodding head of the mother, the child's tireless insolence.

Gina forces her eyes to scan the faces of the other passengers. If they have noticed anything they have decided against bearing witness.

Cardboard cut-outs. The book had said, The soldier's eyes were dark holes, empty. Yours too, thought Gina. She recalled the experience of being a tiny child: if you did not want a thing to exist, you averted your eyes. When you grow up, the trick no longer works.

But for the passengers it is a comfort.

Gina tries their route of escape. She looks out on to the passing landscape, of green hills whose sides erosion has ripped away to reveal naked chalk; different from the rolling woodland the bus has just passed through. Gina's brother had once called it Rupert Bear country.

This isn't a Rupert Bear story, thinks Gina. I wish it was.

"Is that so?" That phrase again. This time the mother swings round on full shoulder. She stares at Gina: the same eyes as her child, the same venom. Now two pairs of eyes swallow the space between passengers who have never met before.

Gina raises her book almost to the level of her face. It could be construed as a provocative action, but she does not look up to note the effect upon the conspirators.

Yes, she is defining them as that. It is a plot. To pick on someone. Perhaps anyone.

"And she needn't think that'll make any difference."

Though the page of the book is nearer, the words are blurred. Your hand is shaking. You cannot hold it at this level and stop it shaking.

Read!

The soldier's knock has sounded in the night. He waits. The rain has flattened his hair upon his skull; his clothes have shrunk about his limbs. He is enough to scare the dead.

Gina attempts to counter the words on the page: Rupert Bear, Rupert Bear, safe and smiling in red jersey and yellow check pants.

Read!

"We'll do something about it, don't fret."

Read! But what's this fiction compared to these characters one arm's reach away? Gina thinks, maybe fiction is what happens to other people. This mother and her kid want me dead. Perhaps I remind them of somebody who once did them harm.

As if in recognition of her hysteria, and to subdue it by meeting it head on, Gina looks up swiftly.

"There!"

And the mother echoes the child, loud enough for the whole bus to hear.

"Sure, love, sure!"

Again, whispering.

I do not know you.

Read. It is probably all in your imagination.

The whisper has no end. It grows on itself, issuing coils out of nothing.

In the story, the door of the end-terrace cottage has opened on to darkness – and eyes; not of the young woman as the soldier expects, but of a dog springing from the recesses of the room.

Yet thank God. The bus is coming to a stop – their stop, mother and child. The girl refuses Gina the blessing of her back, of her retreat. She stands, turns, stares. She challenges Gina to look; forces her to look.

The shock of the eyes is as intense as it is unjust: why me? And the face that frames the eyes is grizzled, an old woman's face. Like those swathed in black shawls they show of Lebanon after the bombs, after the bodies have strewn the city pavements; after the incendiaries have burnt the victims out of recognition.

Eyes accusing the whole world.

The mother has reached the steps. She descends. The girl has waited her moment. The bus mirror reflects the mother's journey. The girl faces Gina.

"We know who *you* are!"

The girl thrusts out her tongue. A snake, skin-shorn, a quivering spear of a tongue. Then she follows her mother down.

The relief is immense. It's over. It's happened to me alone, though up here I'm not alone. Gina takes in the faces of her fellow passengers. Has even one of you noticed, heard? How would they come forward if obliged?

There's never no smoke without fire, my dear.

She heads back into her book and she finds she has turned two pages at once. It is not the end of the story. Already sensing this, Gina is peering into the round bus mirror which gives a perfect view of the child and her mother on the bus platform. And the child is pointing upwards; up the steps.

Read. Blank out. The bus can't be stopped for ever. The dog has sprung in joyful recognition of the soldier. It is a blind love. The soldier stumbles and the stair passage is all at once filled with the mother returning. In her fury, scrambling up.

The eyes have it.

She is tall and advancing on Gina. She does not hesitate. She strikes Gina in the face. Advances, strikes her, the back of her hand to Gina's cheek and bone, then again with the fingers taut, nails out, she lands a blow downwards and across.

The woman does not speak until she has finished her assault. She is a tower over Gina. "And don't you do that again, Miss, to a girl who's been in hospital... You slut!"

Gina partially deflects a final blow that sends her book skating along the bus floor. "I never..."

The woman wheels about. She spares one glance at the passengers. "Our day out," she cries. "And this happens!" She goes down the stairs to her daughter. Together, they alight from the bus.

Gina does not move. She leaves her book on the floor. She feels the eyes now; their interest, their unspoken accusations. Her face stings, but she will not touch it. She will not acknowledge wounds, not yet, though she may be bleeding and her neck feels ricked.

Cardboard cut-outs. She will not give them that satisfaction. She recovers her book. There is going to be a happy ending, of a sort. Gina reads. She shakes.

Forget it.

A case of...

Be cardboard, like them. It helps. But her whole body is trembling. She watches, helpless, as a tear falls on to the page. For a split second the tear magnifies the letters beneath it as the bus mirror magnified the angry mother. Between them, the tear and the dark print form the pupil of a glaring eye.

For Sophie, to whom something very like this actually happened.
from Make Your Move by James Watson

Discussing the story

1 Note down your first reactions to the story.

2 Did the story develop as you expected? What did you expect
   would happen? Were you pleased or disappointed with what
   actually happened? Why? *If you are working as a group, note down
   any differences in people's responses.*

3 At the end of the story, James Watson claims that he wrote it
   from real life. Do you believe him? What details can you find
   that help the story to sound realistic?

4 What part do the other passengers on the bus play in the story?
   How do their reactions affect the story?

5 We never hear what the girl says to her mother. What effect does
   that have on the story?

6 We also never learn the names of the mother and daughter. How
   does this affect our view of them?

7 In what ways has James Watson built up the tension in his
   story? Did he succeed in keeping you eager to go on reading?

Choosing a title

Often the title of a story is the last part to be written. Sometimes it is also the most difficult part. If you had been James Watson, what would you have called this story?

Look at these seven alternatives (which include the title he actually chose).

1 For what reasons might you choose each title?

2 Can you suggest one or two more of your own?

3 Which titles do you prefer? Choose a favourite and two reserves.

The Return

Games With Strangers

Cardboard Cut-Outs

Smoke Without Fire

The Eyes Have It

Faceless   **Is That So?**

Stories within stories

There are two distinct stories within James Watson's tale: the one on the bus and the one in the book that Gina is reading.

1 What do we hear of the soldier's tale? Make brief notes, starting like this:

soldier   *after war*   *face is grotesque: bomb*   *coming home*

2 What links can you see between the two stories?

3 What reasons can you find for the presence of the soldier's story within the main story?

TEACHER'S PACK 4

Possible responses to these questions are available in **Heinemann English Teacher's Pack 4**, together with the title that James Watson actually chose for his story.

Options for writing

Gina writes a letter to a close friend in which she tells her about what has happened to her on the bus...
Remember to include not just an account of what happened but also Gina's feelings about the incident.

Look back at the story Gina was reading on the bus. Using that information and adding further material of your own, complete the tale.

Write your own story in which a person is victimised for something they have not done.
In your planning, think about how much you are going to explain and how much you will leave shrouded in mystery and doubt.

Write a story about the effects on someone of two other people whispering and laughing about him or her. Set the story in a primary/middle school or in the first two years of your current school.

FOR STARTERS

Do you judge a book by its cover? Or its opening page?

This unit looks at both and explores what you can learn from them about the contents of the book and about whether you are likely to enjoy it or not.

Look first at the covers.

- What impression of the book do they give?
- Do they give you a clue about the genre of writing?
- Do they give any clues to what will happen in the novel?
- Match the covers with the openings of the novels which follow.

> *Genre*
> The type or category in which a book might be placed: for instance, science fiction, fantasy, romance, thriller and mystery.

Book A

In a corner of the Hall of Harmony a woman was playing the harp. She sat on a raised platform so that everybody could see her, as well as hear her.

The watchers were all sick, all waiting, all hoping. In the next hour something marvellous might happen and they would be sick no longer. They listened in silence to the gentle notes of the harp.

One of them was different from the others. All the rest had come to the Foundation because they were sick, and were hoping to be healed. But one young man had made himself sick in order to come here. He too was waiting and hoping, but for something else.

Book B

Heat the colour of fire, sky as heavy as mud, and under both the soil – hard, dry, unyielding.

It was a silent harvest. Across the valley, yellow rice fields stretched, stooped and dry. The sun glazed the afternoon with a heat so fierce that the distant mountains shimmered in it. The dust in the sky, the cracked earth, the shrivelled leaves fluttering on brittle branches – everything was scorched.

Fanning out in a jagged line across the fields were the harvesters, their sickles flashing in the sun. Nobody spoke. Nobody laughed. Nobody sang. The only noise was wave after wave of sullen hisses as the rice stalks were slashed and flung to the ground.

Book C

progris riport 1 martch 3

Dr Strauss says I should rite down what I think and remembir and evrey thing that happins to me from now on. I dont no why but he says its importint so they will see if they can use me. I hope they use me becaus Miss Kinnian says mabye they can make me smart. I want to be smart. My name is Charlie Gordon I werk in Donners bakery where Mr Donner gives me 11 dollers a week and bred or cake if I want. I am 32 yeres old and next munth is my brithday. I tolld dr Strauss and perfesser Nemur I cant rite good but he says it dont matter he says I shud rite just like i talk and like I rite compushishens in Miss Kinnians class at the beekmin collidge center for retarted adults where I go to lern 3 times a week on my time off. Dr. Strauss says to rite a lot evrything I think and evrything that happins to me but I cant think anymor becaus I have nothing to rite so I will close for today...yrs truly Charlie Gordon.

Book D

"Little Man, would you come on? You keep it up and you're gonna make us late."

My youngest brother paid no attention to me. Grasping more firmly his newspaper-wrapped notebook and his tin-can lunch of cornbread and oil sausages, he continued to concentrate on the dusty road. He lagged several feet behind my other brothers, Stacey and Christopher-John, and me, attempting to keep the rusty Mississippi dust from swelling with each step and drifting back upon his shiny black shoes and the cuffs of his corduroy pants by lifting each foot high before setting it gently down again. Always meticulously neat, six-year-old Little Man never allowed dirt or tears or stains to mar anything he owned. Today was no exception.

Book E

May 20th

I am afraid.

Someone is coming.

That is, I think someone is coming, though I am not sure, and I pray that I am wrong. I went into the church and prayed all this morning. I sprinkled water in front of the altar, and put some flowers on it, violets and dogwood.

But there is smoke. For three days there has been smoke, not like the time before. That time, last year, it rose in a great cloud a long way away, and stayed in the sky for two weeks. A forest fire in the dead woods, and then it rained and the smoke stopped. But this time it is a thin column, like a pole, not very high.

Book F

In the days when the spinning-wheels hummed busily in the farmhouses – and even great ladies, clothed in silk and threadlace, had their toy spinning-wheels of polished oak – there might be seen in districts far away among the lanes, or deep in the bosom of the hills, certain pallid undersized men, who, by the side of the brawny country-folk, looked like the remnants of a disinherited race. The shepherd's dog barked fiercely when one of these alien-looking men appeared on the upland, dark against the early winter sunset; for what dog likes a figure bent under a heavy bag? – and these pale men rarely stirred abroad without that mysterious burden. The shepherd himself, though he had good reason to believe that the bag held nothing but flaxen thread, or else the long rolls of strong linen spun from that thread, was not quite sure that this trade of weaving, indispensable though it was, could be carried on entirely without the help of the Evil One.

Preparing for discussion

The opening pages are crucial for authors because it is where they will interest or lose their potential readers. In view of this, it is very important to give the reader clear signals about what they can expect. It is equally vital to give readers something to wonder about so that they will keep turning the pages to find out exactly what is happening.

Look at these notes that were made during a discussion of the opening of Book A.

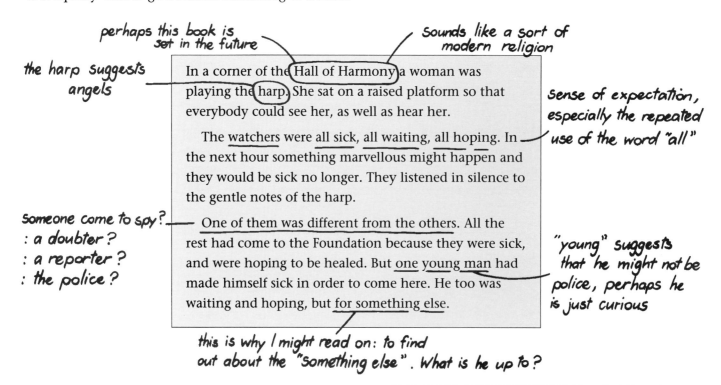

perhaps this book is set in the future

Sounds like a sort of modern religion

the harp suggests angels

In a corner of the Hall of Harmony a woman was playing the harp. She sat on a raised platform so that everybody could see her, as well as hear her.

The watchers were all sick, all waiting, all hoping. In the next hour something marvellous might happen and they would be sick no longer. They listened in silence to the gentle notes of the harp.

One of them was different from the others. All the rest had come to the Foundation because they were sick, and were hoping to be healed. But one young man had made himself sick in order to come here. He too was waiting and hoping, but for something else.

Sense of expectation, especially the repeated use of the word "all"

Someone come to spy?
: a doubter?
: a reporter?
: the police?

"young" suggests that he might not be police, perhaps he is just curious

this is why I might read on: to find out about the "something else". What is he up to?

Discussing the openings

1 Choose two of the openings.

2 What do you learn about the books? Look for clues on any of the following:
   - setting
   - characters
   - narrator
   - genre.

   Distinguish between what you can be certain about and what you read between the lines.

3 What is there in the openings that might encourage a person to read further?

4 Which book would you prefer to start reading and why?

To be continued

Choose the opening that interests you most and write the next few paragraphs of the story. Try to capture the style and feel of the opening. You do not have to explain everything or finish the story, just carry it on a little further.

My kind of book

Prepare a short speech for the rest of your group on the following:

- The type of book covers which attract your attention. Try to find some examples of them.
- The books you would recommend to a friend.
- The books you are reading at the moment and what you think of them.

THE MAN
IN THE LIFT

On the desk in front of me is a pile of essays that I've stopped marking. The reason is the piece of work on top: the one I've just read. Of course, there may be nothing to worry about. I know well enough that the author has a wilder imagination than most.

Ronald Jefferies. If I had to fill in one of those character reference forms for him, I'd probably start with "gifted but odd" or "odd but gifted"; it depends which angle you view him from. And as for his latest offering – do I put a mark on the end of it, together with an appropriate ironic comment, or do I admit that it troubles me and I don't know what to do about it?

One more time. I'll read it once more, and then I shall be certain.

"I'm in my bedroom. The door's closed, which means I'm supposed to be doing my homework. Somewhere downstairs Mum and Dad are watching television, and Karen's gone to the youth club with her friends. I remember when I was thirteen playing ping-pong seemed vaguely exciting, a sort of escape, so I don't take the mickey out of her.

I should be writing a timed essay for English which is why I've got the alarm-clock next to me. I bought it at a jumble sale, from the White Elephant stall. It's chrome-plated and I shined it up when I got home. 'American Alarms. Patent Pending. 1908' it says on the back. It's got this amazingly frantic bell too. But I don't use it as an alarm-clock. The tick's too loud. Keeps me awake half the night, and at the moment I seem to do that well enough without any assistance.

Why? Because I think I'm in trouble; and that's something I normally manage to steer clear of: I keep my eyes and ears open, I can run quite fast and, if the worst comes to the worst, I do a pretty good line in grovelling. Say the Fifth Year thugs corner you behind the dustbins. If you say the right things and hand over the money for them to buy another pack of Marlboro, they generally give you a reprieve. So long as you don't try to sound too smart. 'Actually' is a word to avoid. I've only used it the once. 'Where do you think you're going, Jefferies?' 'Well, actually –' I didn't even manage to finish the sentence before I was grabbed. Still, you learn from your mistakes. Now, I'd never antagonise a neanderthal with vocabulary.

But those characters never gave me sleepless nights. It was the trip to the Barbican that did it; the school trip to *Macbeth*.

Methought I heard a voice cry "Sleep no more!
Macbeth does murder sleep."

Ironic that.

The play itself was great. Dark. Claustrophobic. Everything closing in on Macbeth, even the scenery, so that by the end it's as if he's physically trapped in a little box.

The only problem was that they played the whole thing without an interval, so as soon as the applause had died down, everyone flooded out and into the toilets. My seat was bang in the middle of the circle so I was one of the last out, and by the time I'd finished, the rest of my party had disappeared.

That left me with a dilemma: either I waited where I was until someone realised I was missing; or I tried to find my way back to the coach alone. The trouble is that I have no sense of direction at all, and the Barbican is built like a multi-dimensional maze. You're supposed to work out where you're going by following a yellow line painted on the ground, like Theseus and his ball of string! This takes you up steps, down steps, along walkways, past doors into tower-block flats, round a floodlit church that's presumably there only because someone wouldn't let them knock it down, and, if you're very lucky, out into the streets of London. I didn't much fancy my chances of making it, to be honest, but it seemed so feeble just to stand there and wait that I left the theatre and set off along the nearest walkway.

For a while I even felt I knew where I was going, but the feeling didn't last long. I'd hoped to keep my bearings by the church in the centre of the whole complex, but soon even that had vanished and I found myself bumbling round walkways I'd not seen on the way *into* the theatre, and on completely the wrong level. I checked my watch by one of the yellowish lights at the entrance to a block of flats. Fifteen minutes since the performance ended. The others would be sitting on the coach and cries of 'Where the hell's Jefferies got to? Bloody typical!' would be starting up. Meantime, here I was scooting round the Barbican like a headless chicken.

At this point I decided it might be sensible to go back to the theatre and hang around until some irate teacher came to find me – and sod the humiliation. Then I realised I no longer knew where the theatre was either. The only solution was to step into the nearest block of flats and ask someone for directions; certainly there was no one around on that God-forsaken walkway.

I must admit that the idea of ringing a doorbell and bursting unknown and unannounced into somebody's evening made me a bit anxious: for some reason I expect strangers to be hostile. So for a moment or two I stood in the entrance hall, dithering near the lift. Just then I heard its winding gear grind into action. The lights above the lift doors showed that it was coming down from several floors above. As I hadn't called it there was presumably a passenger, which solved my problem quite neatly. I could ask *them*.

I watched the light go out as the lift moved between floors, then on, then off again, and still it was heading down to my level. At last I could hear it slowing to a standstill then, as the bell pinged to announce the opening of the doors, a thought struck me. Whoever was about to leave the lift had no idea I was there. If I advanced on them with an 'Excuse me but...' what would they think? Probably that I was a drunk or a mugger. Maybe I should stand well clear and let them get out into the open.

As I was debating all this the doors opened and I found myself staring, not into a surprised face, but at the back wall of the lift. Nobody there at all. Then I looked down towards the floor.

Sitting in the corner with legs stuck straight out in front of him, was a man. Mid forties. Foreign, I thought. His head was tipped forward on to his chest so I couldn't see his face. His hair was black and wiry, greying at the sides. He was breathing erratically. So much for my worrying about being taken for a drunk. The drunk was in the lift and spark out for the night! Better leave him where he was and try the next block of flats.

Just then his eyes flicked open and he stared straight at me. Very slowly his hand came up off the floor and he beckoned. I was rooted to the spot. Then he mumbled something. I couldn't hear what it was so I stepped into the lift; it rocked slightly on its winding cable. The expression on the man's face was horrible. It was like a mixture of pain and pleading. And he was still holding out his hand towards me. In it I could suddenly make out the edge of a piece of paper. Without thinking what I was doing, I reached down to take it from him. He nodded as if to encourage me, and the pain on his face seemed to double.

As I pulled the paper from his grip I heard the thud of the door mechanism. I was about to be trapped in the lift with him. I panicked, whirled around and struck blindly at the panel of buttons on the lift wall. Somehow I managed to hit 'Open Door' and, after a second's hesistation, the doors moved apart again and I jumped out. That was when I heard footsteps on the nearby stairs. Someone was in a great hurry, half running, half jumping, and the clattering of their feet was getting rapidly louder.

By this time the lift was on the move again. The lights above it started blinking, and the footsteps were coming down faster than the lift was going up. Suddenly I decided to do what I was best at. I thrust open the entrance door and ran like a madman.

Even then, part of me was curious to know what the hell was going on: to stop under one of the lights and take a look at the piece of paper; to turn round and catch a glimpse of whoever was running after me – because, by now, I knew that's what they were doing. Behind me I'd heard the door open and feet pound on to the walkway. More than one pair by the sound of it. Fortunately, my feet kept thinking for me. On I ran, though I'd no idea where I was going. There seemed to be no way off that particular level.

Then suddenly I was at the top of some steps; and there was the lit-up church – which meant that a couple of flights down and just over to the left would be...yes, there it was: a large terrace and, behind it, the lights of the theatre foyer.

I was breathing heavily as I landed on the terrace, lost my balance for a moment and stumbled. Before I could straighten up I heard more footsteps, this time from the side and bearing down on me fast. At that point I was so confused I nearly turned round and ran straight back up the steps.

'Jefferies, what in God's name do you think you're playing at?'

Normally the dulcet tones of Mr Roberts getting annoyed don't appeal to me, but now I was so relieved to see him, they were music to my ears.

'Well?' he said, as I still hadn't answered his question.

'I got lost, sir,' I told him.

'Nothing like stating the obvious,' he said. 'Well, you score ten for honesty, nothing for imagination and bonus marks for sheer stupidity.'

'Yes, sir,' I agreed. 'Shall we go now?'

'What a good idea, Jefferies. I presume you'd like me to lead off.'

'Yes, sir. Thank you, sir.'

As we made our way through and out of the maze, I glanced round every now and then, but there was no sign of anyone following. No sound, either, except for Mr Roberts venting his annoyance: 'I waited ten minutes on the coach. Pure optimism, of course, but at the time it seemed preferable to carting the quarter of a mile back to the theatre. Honestly, if you didn't know the way back, why didn't you stick with one of the group?'

'They all left before me, sir.'

He lapsed into sullen silence for the rest of the walk. As we reached the coach the lads on the back seat saw us and started cheering. Old Roberts studiously avoided seeing the gestures a couple of them were making. 'Right, let's get you on board and be gone,' he said.

I took the applause and the jeering well enough. Even managed a little bow. Unfortunately, the only available seat was near the back, just in front of the lads, so the journey home was a bit of a trial. What annoyed me more than anything, though, was the fact that I couldn't take out the piece of paper while they were pestering me. In fact, it wasn't till I was home and getting ready for bed that I had a chance to look at it properly. It turned out to be a small piece of lined paper, with holes at the side, presumably out of something like a Filofax. And the only thing written on it was a series of numbers.

There were seven digits and, strange as it may seem, I didn't twig straight away what they meant. It was only as I was lying in bed that night that I realised it must be a London phone number. If you live outside London you get used to seeing the code in front, and whoever had written this had left the 071 off. The other thing that struck me then was that it ought to have been written in two blocks: three digits then four. This list of numbers was continuous, as if the writer had heard them spoken, rather than copying them from a directory.

Pure speculation, and probably idle speculation at that. But I spent a long time looking at that piece of paper before I turned the light off, till I not only knew the number by heart; I could picture every twist and flick of the pen, the tiny angled cross-bar on the seven. By the time I went to sleep I could have produced a perfect copy, even with my eyes closed.

The next day I found I couldn't concentrate too well on lessons. Old Roberts, predictably enough, had us discussing the previous night's performance. Did we feel the witches were presented as active forces of evil, rather than merely prophets of doom, etc. Normally I'd have joined in, and he must have realised my mind was elsewhere because he said, 'Feeling a little jaded today, Jefferies? Too much unaccustomed exercise last night, no doubt.' But he was so enthusiastic about his own ideas that he soon forgot me, and I was free to mull over my problem. Problems, rather. As I saw it, there were five.

One: why had I been given the piece of paper?

Two: what had happened to the man in the lift after I ran away?

Three: who had been running after me, and why?

Four: what was their connection with the man?

Five: – and most important of all: what the hell was I supposed to do now?

As I couldn't answer any of the first four questions there seemed only one logical answer to the final one. But I didn't get round to making the call until late that evening. I had to wait till the rest of the family was safely occupied. It was just after nine forty.

As the ringing tone began my heart was beating at double speed. What exactly was I going to say, for heaven's sake? 'I'm phoning because a complete stranger gave me this number, and by the way can you tell me what's happened to him?' My nerve held out for ten rings, then I put the phone down. At least I'd tried. And perhaps my not getting through was an omen: 'Leave well alone; just screw up the piece of paper and throw it in the bin.'

But I didn't, and that night I hardly slept at all.

Next evening I tried again. This time it was earlier, and I was given no opportunity to change my mind. The phone at the other end was picked up almost immediately.

Voice: Hello?

Me: Excuse me, but I think you might be able to help me. I was given your number by somebody.

Voice: (*Suspiciously*) This is an ex-directory number. Who gave it to you?

Me: I don't know his name. I was hoping you could tell me because, well, the thing is, he seemed pretty ill when he gave it to me.

Voice: (*After a pause*) Ill?

Me: Yes – at least he looked that way to me. I found him in a lift.

Voice: In the lift – yes, of course. Look, it's very thoughtful of you to phone like this. I should explain. It was my brother you met. He has a heart condition. Quite serious. In fact, he was very lucky the other night. We found him in time to get him to hospital. He's still there, otherwise, I'm sure he'd want to thank you himself for phoning.

Me: Oh – well, he's all right then?

Voice: Yes, yes. He'll need to rest, of course... I presume he gave you the number so you could call for help.

Me: I'm afraid I didn't do too well then. I'm only two days late.

Voice: (*Laughing*) Not to worry. As it happened, things worked out fine.

As far as I was concerned, that should have been the end of the call, but he carried on talking to me for a while about nothing in particular, pointing out several times how grateful his brother would be. I was on my guard in case he said something like 'If you give me your number I'll get him to thank you personally.' But he didn't. Eventually, he stopped quite abruptly, said 'thank you' for the nth time, and put the phone down.

For the rest of the evening I paced round the house: the phone call had given me the creeps and I couldn't settle to anything. I suppose what I'd been told was just about plausible – if you discounted the running footsteps as coincidence – but one thing really bothered me. If, as he said, his brother had nearly died a couple of nights ago, the man I'd spoken to had no right to sound so calm about it. Relieved, yes; that I could have understood. But completely detached and emotionless? We could just as easily have been discussing the price of cheese, or how to polish a pair of shoes.

And how had I sounded to him? Hopefully, as if I believed him. That night I stayed up late, reading. When I finally put out the light it was two a.m. Even then, I slept badly.

All this was two nights ago, since when nothing has happened; not in the strict sense of the word. But I have two good reasons for worry. Firstly, I think I'm being watched.

Despite the insomnia, I've found I can get some sleep so long as I make myself physically exhausted. So, when the others are asleep, in the small hours of the morning, I very quietly leave the house and go for a long walk. And for two nights in a row there's been a car I've not seen before parked a little way down on the other side of the road. Someone's sitting in the driving seat and both times I've walked past he's been consulting a map or something. When I come back, about half an hour later, the car has gone.

Secondly, I discovered something in the paper this morning – I've been keeping my eyes open for the past few days: a short article about some foreign journalist. Seems he's written various things his government doesn't like, they've put the screws on him and he's come to this country for some kind of safety. Now he's gone missing and nobody knows where. There's a

rather blurred photograph too, not a particularly recent one either, but clear enough for me.

When I look back over what I've written in the last hour, what amazes me is how much you can write when it actually means something to you. As opposed to *Macbeth: the Anatomy of Terror*, which is what I should have been writing about.

Though, in a strange way, maybe I have."

It's that last remark which makes me question the whole thing. Provocative and tongue-in-cheek. Typical Jefferies. Give him any task and he'll find the most unusual way of doing it. Never orthodox. Never point A to point B like other people.

So what *has* he been writing about? The build-up of fear; the onset of paranoia, when everyone and everything is seen as threatening; the loss of reason and the torment of imagination. Well, they're all there in *Macbeth*, so maybe I should write: "As a fictional foray into the realms of the disturbed mind, this is probably worthy of a place in the school magazine. As an examination of the text it is, as you well know, complete rubbish." And having soothed his ego with the school magazine reference, I'd give him nought out of twenty.

So why don't I?

Partly because I'm in a unique position to verify the truth of much of his story. I was the one who went back to find him at the Barbican; he was certainly out of breath when I found him, and somewhat ill at ease; my remarks at the time are recorded more or less verbatim, as is my comment to him in the English lesson; on the two occasions I saw him subsequently he appeared tired and distant.

I realise, of course, that by embroidering a fictional tale with threads of fact, the whole thing is made to sound more believable and he is a sophisticated enough boy to realise this also. The 'disappearing journalist' is also fact. I read it myself in the Sunday paper.

All this I can explain away, if with some difficulty. Two things remain. Jefferies handed in his 'essay' yesterday, Monday. Today he was absent from my lesson and, as it transpired when I later checked the register, had been absent all day. More significant perhaps is the small piece of lined paper attached to his work. On it is written a sequence of numbers, in a hand that seems to me very different from Jefferies', judging by the figures used when dating his work, for example.

Therein, I suppose, lies the answer. If this is an elaborate hoax and Jefferies is having a bit of a laugh at my expense – at my gullibility – then the proof lies in the phone number.

I shall dial it and find out.

Rex Harley

Developing a thriller

On the cassette that accompanies this book, Rex Harley talks about the process of writing this story and his novel **Black November.**

Short stories in the thriller genre such as **The Man in the Lift** are quite rare. One of the reasons for that is the fact that it usually takes time to build up a sense of tension and fear. One of the most important techniques in thriller writing is to keep the reader waiting and wondering what will happen. Which parts of the story do you think help to develop a sense of tension?

The moment the teacher says, "there may be nothing to worry about" you immediately suspect that there is.

Fact or fiction?

Mr Roberts, the English teacher, is not certain whether Jefferies' essay is fact or fiction.

1 What do you think?
2 What evidence is there in the story to support your view?

Five problems

The day after the visit to the theatre Jefferies is thinking about what has happened and comes up with five problems. The final one (about what he can do) he answers by making the telephone call. The other four remain unsolved:

> One: why had I been given the piece of paper?
>
> Two: what had happened to the man in the lift after I had run away?
>
> Three: who had been running after me and why?
>
> Four: what was their connection with the man?

1 In groups, find as many explanations for these problems as you can.

2 Decide which explanations seem most likely to you.

From story to video

Suppose that a film company wants to turn Rex Harley's short story into a television programme. In your group discuss:

1 What scenes from the story might work well on television?

2 What scenes might be less interesting unless changes were made?

3 What additional scenes might be needed?

4 Produce a storyboard for the part of the story in which Ronald Jefferies first notices the lift. As a start, the first two frames are given below:

Mid shot of Jefferies looking vaguely around entrance hall of the flats		SOUND clanking of lift as it starts up
Shot of open doors with man in the lift		SOUND Clanking of lift doors

Write a filmscript for this part of the story, based on your storyboard.

Scene number

(15) ENTRANCE HALL. ——— *location*
RONALD IS STANDING IN THE MIDDLE. HE APPEARS TO BE
UNCERTAIN ABOUT WHAT TO DO NEXT. *actions* (SOUND OF LIFT)
CAMERA PANS FROM RONALD TO DOORS OF LIFT. *sounds*
CAMERA PULLS BACK SO THAT LIFT FLOOR INDICATOR IS VISIBLE.
LIGHT ON INDICATOR MOVES FROM 9 DOWNWARDS.
CAMERA FOCUSES ON LIFT INDICATOR. *suggestions for*
RONALD: That's it. *camera shots*

Speech

EXTENSIONS

1 What happens when Mr Roberts makes the telephone call? Continue the story from that point.
Try to write an ending that leaves a reader wanting more just as Rex Harley did.

2 What has happened to Ronald Jefferies? Let him tell his own story from the moment the essay was handed in. You do not have to explain every tiny detail of what has happened or finish with all the loose ends tidied up.

FILMSCRIPT AND STORYBOARDS

Further help and advice on preparing filmscript and storyboards can be found in **Heinemann English Assessment and Reference File**, pages 95 to 99.

PUNISHED FOR *YOUR LANGUAGE*

Ever since Daniel Defoe published **The Journal of a Plague Year** in 1722, writers have used the format of a diary for fiction. It is very effective because it makes you feel close to the person telling the story. Often, it can make a story sound immensely believable. This is particularly useful for writers who are basing their story on actual experiences.

The extracts that follow are from the opening pages of Rafik Schami's novel **A Handful of Stars.** The banning of Arabic in the monastery to make the students learn French actually happened. How much of the rest is based on real life, you can decide for yourself.

January 25th

I want to jot down what our quarter in Damascus looks like. My parents have moved three times since I was born, and I no longer know exactly how the previous houses looked. The street we live on now is rather narrow. It is in the eastern part of the city. Near my house is St Paul's Chapel. Many tourists visit the place from which the apostle took off and went to Europe.

Our houses are built of clay. Several families live in each one, and every building has an interior courtyard, which belongs to all the families who live in it; here they come together to talk and laugh and sometimes to quarrel. The adults keep to the courtyard. The street belongs to the children, the beggars, and to itinerant pedlars. Every house has two storeys; the roofs are flat and almost all the same height, so you can walk from one roof to another without any trouble.

I still remember the morning we were sitting on the terrace eating breakfast, when suddenly a young man peered down from the roof. He wanted to know where the door to the house was. My mother showed him. He leapt onto our terrace and from there ran to the stairs and out into the alley.

My mother was just bringing the teapot from the kitchen when two policemen suddenly appeared.

"Have you seen a young Palestinian?" one of them asked.

"A Palestinian? No! Have you no shame, forcing your way into our house! There are women and children here!" she cried out.

The policeman apologised, and both of them turned to go. My mother went on eating her breakfast as if nothing had happened. Her behaviour astonished me.

In the afternoon I just had to ask her, "Why did you lie?"

"The young man looked very worried. He has a mother, and she wouldn't report you if you were running away from the police!"

"And how do you know that? Are you sure?"

"Yes, I'm sure. I'm a mother." She smiled and kissed me on the forehead.

جليف

Rafik Schami's house in Damascus

A street in Damascus

February 10th

I have three friends: Uncle Salim, who is seventy-five years old; Mahmud, who is fifteen; and Josef, who is exactly my age.

For most of his life Uncle Salim drove a coach, so he tells great stories about robbers, kings and fairies. He has seen a lot and has survived several famous robbers and kings and, yes, perhaps fairies as well. Uncle Salim, Mahmud and I all live in the same house. Josef's house is just opposite ours.

Mahmud and Josef have never been outside Syria. I have. I spent two years in a monastery in Lebanon. My father sent me there to make a priest out of me. Every poor family tries to make a son into a clergyman, because a priest commands respect and gives the family a good reputation. After two years I gave it up.

The pupils came from various Arab countries, but we were forced to speak French. So each newcomer had to take a crash course in that language, and then, after two months, he was no longer permitted to speak a single word of Arabic. If he did, he was given a small, round piece of wood, with the letter S (which stood for signal) on it. He had to hide it on his person and secretly wait for some new victim to foist if off on. If he betrayed himself in any way, the other pupils would know he had the signal and avoid him like a skunk. No, he had to accept it quietly and slink around until someone or other unsuspectingly spoke Arabic in his presence. In this way, we were all educated as little spies. Whoever was last to possess the wooden disk had to eat his supper kneeling.

Having the signal was an odd feeling I will never forget. It seemed very warm in your pocket and gave you power over the others. If you got it early enough in the day, you had a lot of leeway. I showed mercy if my would-be victim was someone I liked. But I'd press it gleefully into the hand of an arse-licker. After a while, secret gangs formed. I belonged to one made up of five students. We vowed to help one another. You couldn't slip the wooden disk to anyone in the gang, so if one of us had it, the other four basked in

security and made full use of the opportunity to speak Arabic.

One of the priests got wind of our gang and railed against using the signal for turning the pupils against one another. But he was laughed off the teaching staff, and the war of the gangs went on.

Some gangs evolved into commandos; members even took the signal at their own peril when it fell into the hands of a less brave member of their gang. Then they would go searching for a victim. Supper was around six, and it was considered a heroic act to take the thing into your possession with only an hour left. One of these kamikazes, an Egyptian, pressed it into the hand of a teacher when the teacher said in Arabic, at a quarter to six, that he was dying of hunger. The other teachers gazed into his palm, stunned. Then they announced the rule against speaking Arabic didn't apply to them; teachers were not part of the game. And so on this evening the little Egyptian had to eat kneeling. This was the first time the pupils showed respect to anyone who had to do so. We pressed his shoulder as we passed by.

March 20th

Mr Katib is a fantastic teacher. His predecessor taught us to fear and respect language; Mr Katib teaches us to love it. Earlier we had been told that imagination resided in exaggeration alone, but Mr Katib teaches us that fairy tales transpire in the simple events of our everyday lives. Our previous teacher never let us describe the fragrance of flowers or the flight of swallows. All he ever wanted us to write about were fabulous banquets, birthdays and experiences. But not a single one of us from impoverished homes has ever experienced an exceptional birthday or a great feast.

I will never forget the pupil who, in my opinion, wrote the best composition. We were supposed to describe a banquet. When guests come – and they often appear out of nowhere – my mother shares everything she has with them. My mother always cooks so much, I think she is constantly expecting visitors. When we have guests, we eat with them, and in their honour my father drinks two glasses of arrack, to be sure the guests will join him in a drink.

Had I described truthfully, I would not even have got a D on my composition. So I went running to Uncle Salim, because he had taken many rich people to celebrations and parties in his coach. Once there, he would often sneak into the kitchen and eat with the cooks and the house staff. He could describe exactly what was served and how, the beverages people drank, and everything they talked about. A few pashas and princes, which no longer exist in Syria, came marching into Uncle Salim's stories, but I replaced them with the chief of police and even a

judge (no judge has ever seen the inside of our apartment!). I wrote that my mother served them a roasted gazelle, stuffed with almonds, rice, and raisins. And of course I recounted the words of praise the judge uttered about my parents' meal and the arrack. It was funny to have only a bit of dry bread in my knapsack during recess and to tell about roast gazelle. None of my schoolmates laughed. They just stared at me with their mouths open. I got a B and listened, just as much a zombie, to the stories of others, in which bishops, generals, poets and traders suddenly joined hands in our poverty-stricken dwellings.

Chalil alone did not play along. When it was his turn, he told the story of what had happened when he asked his parents what a banquet was. His mother immediately went into raptures, at the same time bemoaning her bad luck in having married such a poor man, despite having been courted, when she was young, by many richer suitors. His father became hurt and angry; he said he would have been a rich man long ago if he had not had to feed her large and voracious family (twelve siblings, father, mother, and grandfather). A colleague of his had a good wife, and on the same salary as his they had built two houses. Then Chalil's mother yelled at his father that her parents always brought a lot with them when they came and that he would be better off if he didn't buy arrack. Then he could have scraped together the money for a home long ago. His parents argued a long time. Each of us saw our own families reflected in Chalil's.

Chalil ended his report with the following sentence: "In order to keep them from getting a divorce, I have sworn never again to ask my parents about a banquet!"

The teacher gave him an F. "Theme lacking." Chalil did not return the next day or any other. Now he works in an auto repair shop.

Reading closely

1 What do you learn from the diary about the writer's life and his family?

2 Each of the three diary entries has a similar basic organisation which divides the entry into two parts. Describe this structure in your own words.

Discussion material

1 Find arguments for and against what Rafik's mother said to the policeman.

2 What arguments can you see for and against Chalil leaving school?

3 Explain why the letter 'S' is needed for education in the monastery.

4 Decide whether you think the use of the letter 'S' is justified. Work out a clear argument to defend your decision.

5 What influences are there on your use of language? What effect do they have? Think about:
- pressures to learn another language
- pressures to speak with a particular accent
- pressures to avoid slang and "bad" language.

What are the rights and wrongs of these pressures?

Writing a diary

Now it's your turn.

Write an extract of a story in diary form. Your diary can be totally true, partially true or a complete invention. You can write a diary of any chosen character but remember it must be written convincingly from his or her viewpoint. It is usually a good idea to create a character of about your own age. Writing as if you were someone much older is more difficult.

Think about the period of time the diary will cover and about the main events it will describe. Do not try to fit in everything – it will get out of hand.

Ideas
A diary of...
...homework disasters?
...a failed friendship?
...sporting success?
...a school phobic?
...someone as they move schools?
Make your decision!

DRAFTING

To get the most out of your work:

- First draft - keep it readable.

- Review - listen to the comments of others and check it yourself.

- Final draft - produce a revised best-possible version.

SITA AND MARY

Although fashions change in book publishing, there are always people who are interested in reading the story of another person's life. This section looks at how biographies are written and why they have an appeal. It also gives you a chance to write one.

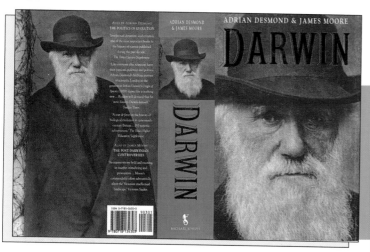

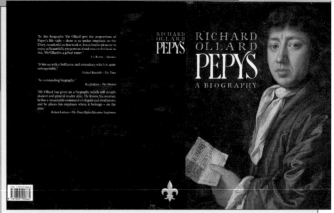

First thoughts

1 Think of three or four people whose life story you would like to read.

2 What is the attraction of the people you have chosen?

3 What would you want to find out about them from their biographies?

4 What makes a biography appealing to read? Think about the way people's lives are portrayed in their biographies.

Preparing a biography

One way of compiling a biography is to work through libraries and old documents. This is the way that historical biographies are usually written. If you are writing about a living person, the story can be discovered through interviews with that person and/or their friends and family.

The two biography extracts which follow have been written after the writers talked to the people whose life stories they were telling. In one case, the writer retells the story in a conventional written form. In the other case, the writer tries to record the story in the way it was spoken. Read both and then decide which is which.

Earrings, ribbons and brothers

When I was about five years old I longed to wear earrings, so I took a long sharp thorn and pushed the point into my ear lobe. It hurt me and the end broke off and stayed in my ear. I never told anyone and it is still there! Soon after I heard that a neighbour was piercing ears with a needle and thread, so I went along and asked her to do mine. Two friends held me still while she pushed the needle through, but it was very painful and I screamed and struggled as she did the other ear. Afterwards I was glad. She left a piece of thread in each hole to keep it open, but now I know that she should have sterilised the needle, as my ears became infected and for some time I had sores on both sides. It was about three months before they cleared up, and when I put my earrings in the infection started again because they were made of cheap metal, not silver, gold or steel. That did not stop me loving to wear earrings, as I still do.

One day my vanity led me into more trouble. Like most Indian girls I had long thick black hair which I wore in a plait. It was the fashion for little girls at that time to wear ribbon bows in white or bright colours in their hair. Some of the better-off children had two plaits and two bows, so I did the same. My eldest brother Krishna was much older than me, and was studying at the university. Because Mother and Father were away a great deal he was head of the house, and with six younger children, five girls and one boy, this was a big responsibility. He took it very seriously and was so strict with us that we feared and disliked him. He often hit us very hard if we annoyed him; if the pots and pans were not clean enough, for instance, or if we were untidy. When he came home that day and saw my plaits he fell into a rage. He seized me, and taking a pair of scissors cut off one plait and threw it over the verandah. Crying from shock and distress I ran down to the courtyard and picked up my lovely plait, still with its ribbon. Now I looked terrible with half my hair cut off close to the scalp.

When Mother came home I ran to show her what he had done and she was angry with Krishna and shouted at him. But he was grown-up and educated and much the cleverest in the family, so he always got the better of her and everyone else. My auntie who was with us at the time said, "Don't worry, all the girls in Delhi are cutting their hair short now, and I will cut the rest of yours." But of course it looked dreadful and I had to wear a veil over my head until it grew. Luckily it grew even longer and glossier than before. When he left home and used to visit us, my brother was quite different, kind and gentle even, but it took us some time to trust him.

Sita Devi
as recorded by Rachel Barton

School, Empire and Fleas

I couldn't write proper, add up. I don't think I was dim, I just thought: There must be better things to do'n this! You could see the teachers thought the same. Some of them, like Miss Farmer, had been there years; they'd grown old and fat so they *hit* you, never moved from their chair, just called you up to the front and gave you a swipe across the head. And the young one! We used to be praps at netball in the front yard, and Miss Salt the young teacher, she always wore a very short gym slip. Up and up she jumped, up and up; she loved jumping! She didn't pay much attention to us, cos by this time a big crowd had gathered on the pavement: chaps going by to the station, the boys from the Commercial school on their way to games. There were whistles and shouts. We never realized it was Miss Salt's limbs, and her lovely attire. *Then* we thought it was us, in our navy blue knickers. But really it was Miss Salt, jumping and jumping; she was the great attraction.

The Vicar came round regular. We all stood up for him, all at once; the classrooms were partitioned with glass, you could see through the whole school. He walked through – if you didn't curtsey you got a swipe off the teacher, after – and then we were allowed to sit down. I used to think: "Why's *e* come?" and "What's it all for?" For example, I weren't too bad at needlework, but you never *made* anything. All you did was stitches, different sorts of fancy stitches, and then you had to unpick them and do some more, with the same bit o' stuff. Naturally, it got black as your hat. Then there was *Empire Day*. They planned weeks in advance for that. The teacher said: "Hewins – Jamaican Banana!" My friend Betty who married Joe Shakespeare was a Tasmanian Apple. Sis? She was lucky; she went to the Board school.

Our mothers did their best: we all had something on our heads, like Christmas crackers. You can imagine some of the boys! Their faces! I had a shift with "*BANANA*" on it, made out of wrapping paper; Betty had cardboard. When the great day came we paraded in the front yard. I was dying of embarrassment. Somebody whispered I'd got "*BANANA*" spelled wrong; I hadn't o'course, but I believed them. We was marched around, then one by one we stood on a platform with a Union Jack draped across, and streamers.

I had to say: "I'm a Jamaican banana." I felt one and all. For once I prayed the boys from the Commercial school wouldn't come by. If anyone giggled they got a swipe. Miss Farmer hit very hard. She leant over the piano stool and she hit you as you marched past. She'd got it off to a fine art.

'The bottling end'
Flowers brewery Stratford-upon-Avon (Late 1930's)

*All dressed up for the brewery
trip Blackpool, 1930's (Mary-centre).*

*Lunch break at the canning factory,
War-time (Mary standing, 3rd from right).*

Once, I remembered, I'd done a sum wrong, so I put a cross. That wouldn't a-been so bad if I'd left it, but I put this cross hard on the paper, ever so hard, spoilt the page. "You spoilt the page!" she shouted. I got a swipe over the head for that. "You spoilt your *book*!" That was exaggerating, but you couldn't argue with the teachers, you couldn't even reason with them. So you can imagine how I was longing and longing for Christmas when I was fourteen.

For the last and the thousandth time Miss Farmer went *Ping*! "'Ere's your note!" And we all sang "God Save the King". Then she said: "Today we 'ave to wish Mary Hewins well in er new career."

Career! Two of the girls were smirking; they'd got their names down at J C Smith's the Draper's. Oh they thought they were something, those two girls. Later, some of the others went to Woolworth's; Woolworth's was coming to Stratford – "*EVERYTHING IN ITS PLACE NOTHING OVER SIXPENCE!*" – and when it did, all the girls who were clever, but not clever enough for Smith's they went there for interview. It was hard to get in; well, the ones they picked were a better class'n me. I wouldn't a-stood a chance.

Mary as Schoolgirl (About 13).

I wasn't dressed like them in those days: we'd got more fleas'n clothes in our house!

I'd wake Jess up: "Ey Jess! There's a flea in bed!"

We lit a candle, tried to catch it. Once you know there's a flea, you can't stop. If it gets you first it'll mark you so's everybody knows. They could tell at school if you'd got fleas: the marks were all round your blooming neck. Mostly they bite on your neck. The girl behind you...oh God.

My looks were alright but you'd got to be – well, a bit posher. J C Smith's could take their pick. And Woolworth's, when they opened. Dora went, and Madge – she was a teacher, after – and the Bromley girls. The Bromleys lived at "Glencoe", in Arden Street, by the school, one of those big houses. They took in lodgers. Madge's Dad was only a baker but they were a bit superior. Woolworth's seemed to go for that type of girl.

Mary Hewins
as told to Angela Hewins

From speech to writing

1 Discuss each passage and decide which writer is trying to keep closest to the spoken word.

2 Now decide exactly what it is that makes one piece of writing look more like the spoken word. What differences can you see between the language of the two extracts?
Think about the following as you read the extracts again:
• accent and dialect
• the use of Standard English
• the use of direct speech
• the length of sentences
• the length of paragraphs
• the use of phrases rather than sentences
• the use of italics and capitals.

HELP

The **Heinemann English Assessment and Reference File** has material about accent, dialect and Standard English on pages 53 to 54.

Facts and feelings

Mary Hewins' memories of school are an interesting combination of facts and feelings about her education. See if you can disentangle the two elements. Use a chart to organise your thoughts into two columns: *facts* and *feelings*.

Writing biography

Now it is your turn to work as biographer to someone. Not everyone will be keen to tell you about their life and most people will have stories that they do not want to tell. You must respect that. On the other hand, many people are more than willing to tell you about their life.

Listen to Angela Hewins describing the way she worked as a biographer, which will help you with this assignment. (Remember that she was dealing with the whole of a person's life and tens of thousands of words. You will only have the time to tell part of a life story.)

S T A G E 1   Who might talk to me?

parents   grandparents   aunts/uncles   neighbours   friends

> **HELP**
>
> Angela Hewins discovered that older people are often more willing to tell their stories and, naturally, have more stories to tell.

S T A G E 2   How do I record it?

- Where?
  Choose a place where the person you are talking to will feel at ease and will not be interrupted every five minutes.

- On tape?
  Some people are put off by a tape recorder but it has the great advantage of recording every word.

- In writing?
  This gives you an immediate written record which can be easier to work from but you can easily miss important points.

S T A G E 3   What questions do I ask?

first memories   school   first job   important moments

what life was like:
food   money   clothes   rules   transport   weather

> **HELP**
>
> Some subjects are easier to remember and to talk about than others. Angela Hewins believes that work, especially the early days, is one of the easiest subjects.

S T A G E 4   How do I organise the material?

- How much will I try to stay close to the spoken word?
- In what order will I tell the story?

DRAFTING

To get the most out of your work:
First draft: keep it readable.
Review: listen to the comments of others and check it yourself.
Final draft: produce a revised best-possible version.

MAKING A TAPE

Hints to help you if you are making a taped interview are available in the **Heinemann English Assessment and Reference File** pages 90, 91 and 92.

THE KID
NEXT DOOR

Pictures often have the power to say more than words. Read this picture story and then work on the activities which follow:

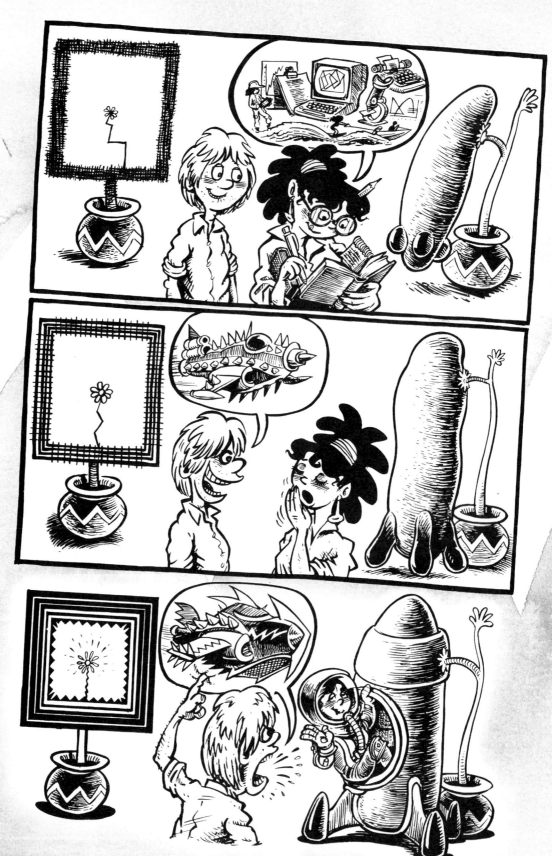

Frame by frame

For most of the strip, each frame is organised in a similar way, with two central characters, each with a speech or thought bubble and each accompanied by a changing "plant".

1 Working in pairs, take each frame in turn and write down one thought or comment for each of the characters depicted. Try to keep your statements very short but closely linked to the images in the speech bubbles.

2 When you have finished the complete strip, take turns in reading your character's thoughts or dialogue to the rest of the group. Decide on those which best fit the pictures.

Potty plants?

In what ways do the two "plants" link with the ideas in the centre of each frame?

1 Why are the "plants" changing in this way?

2 What does each change say about the character it is linked with?

A sense of an ending

The final three frames break away from the format used in the rest of the strip.

1 Why do you think the cartoonist has done this?

2 Do you think it works?

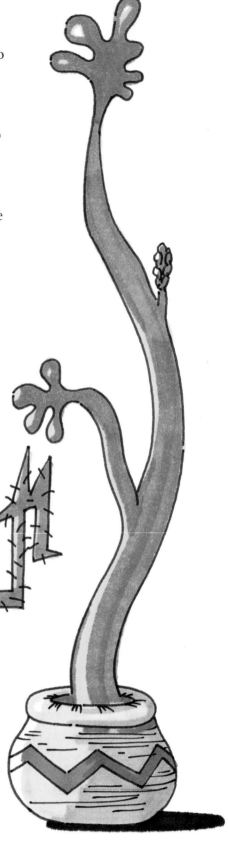

Changes

The Kid Next Door is based on the changes which occur between two
people over a lengthy period of time. Draw a similar story of the
changes in another relationship. For example:
• mother and son
• father and daughter
• teacher and pupil
• doctor and patient
• you and a member of your family.

1 First organise your thoughts by drawing a time-line, showing some of
the major "events" in the lives being depicted – events which might
affect the relationship between the two characters.

2 Next, show through a series of thought or speech bubble images, how
the feelings between your chosen characters change dramatically as a
result of this time-line of events.

Don't worry about your technical
skills as an artist; it is the quality
and originality of your ideas
which count.

THE GREAT TEMPTATION

BUY

Have you ever seen something in a shop which you really wanted but could not afford?

Think about it and how it felt not to be able to have it. Then read the following story by the Italian writer, Italo Calvino.

Marcovaldo at the Supermarket

At six in the evening the city fell into the hands of the consumers. All during the day the big occupation of the productive public was to produce consumer goods. At a certain hour, as if a switch had been thrown, they stopped production and, away!, they were all off, to consume. Every day an impetuous flowering barely had time to blossom inside the lighted shop-windows, the red salamis to hang, the towers of porcelain dishes to rise to the ceiling, the rolls of fabric to unfurl folds like peacock's tails, when lo! the consuming throng burst in, to dismantle, to gnaw, to grope, to plunder. An uninterrupted line wound along all the sidewalks and under the arcades, extended through the glass doors of the shops to all the counters, nudged onwards by each individual's elbows in the ribs of the next, like the steady throb of pistons. Consume! And they touched the goods and put them back and picked them up again and tore them from one another's hands; consume! and they forced the pale salesladies to display on

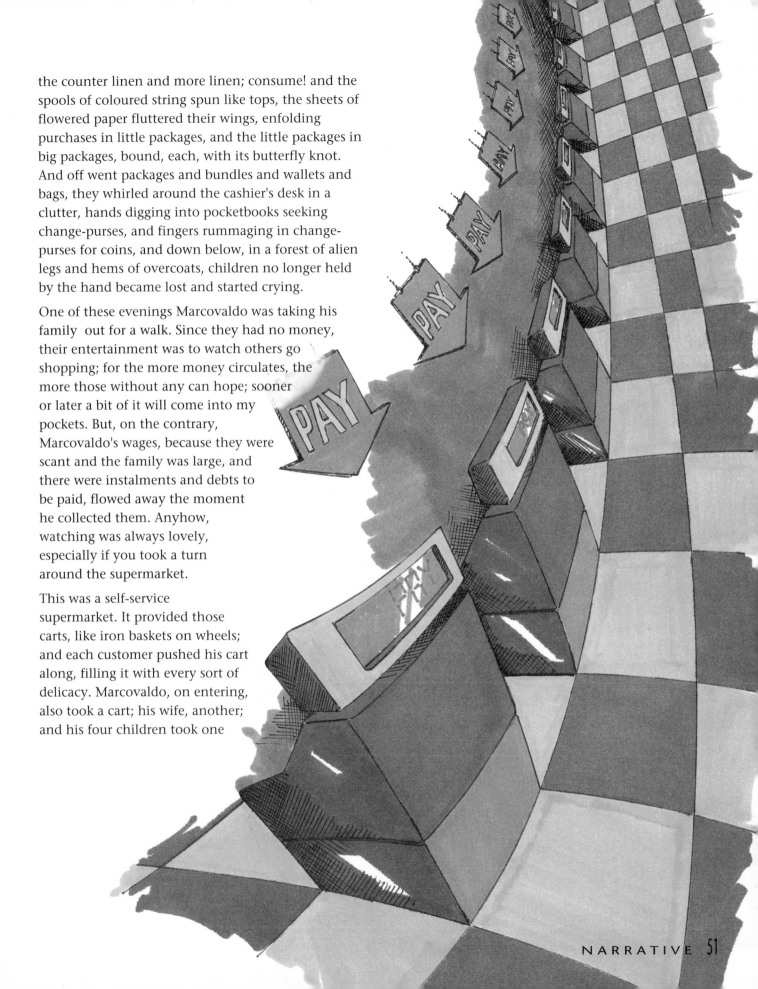

the counter linen and more linen; consume! and the spools of coloured string spun like tops, the sheets of flowered paper fluttered their wings, enfolding purchases in little packages, and the little packages in big packages, bound, each, with its butterfly knot. And off went packages and bundles and wallets and bags, they whirled around the cashier's desk in a clutter, hands digging into pocketbooks seeking change-purses, and fingers rummaging in change-purses for coins, and down below, in a forest of alien legs and hems of overcoats, children no longer held by the hand became lost and started crying.

One of these evenings Marcovaldo was taking his family out for a walk. Since they had no money, their entertainment was to watch others go shopping; for the more money circulates, the more those without any can hope; sooner or later a bit of it will come into my pockets. But, on the contrary, Marcovaldo's wages, because they were scant and the family was large, and there were instalments and debts to be paid, flowed away the moment he collected them. Anyhow, watching was always lovely, especially if you took a turn around the supermarket.

This was a self-service supermarket. It provided those carts, like iron baskets on wheels; and each customer pushed his cart along, filling it with every sort of delicacy. Marcovaldo, on entering, also took a cart; his wife, another; and his four children took one

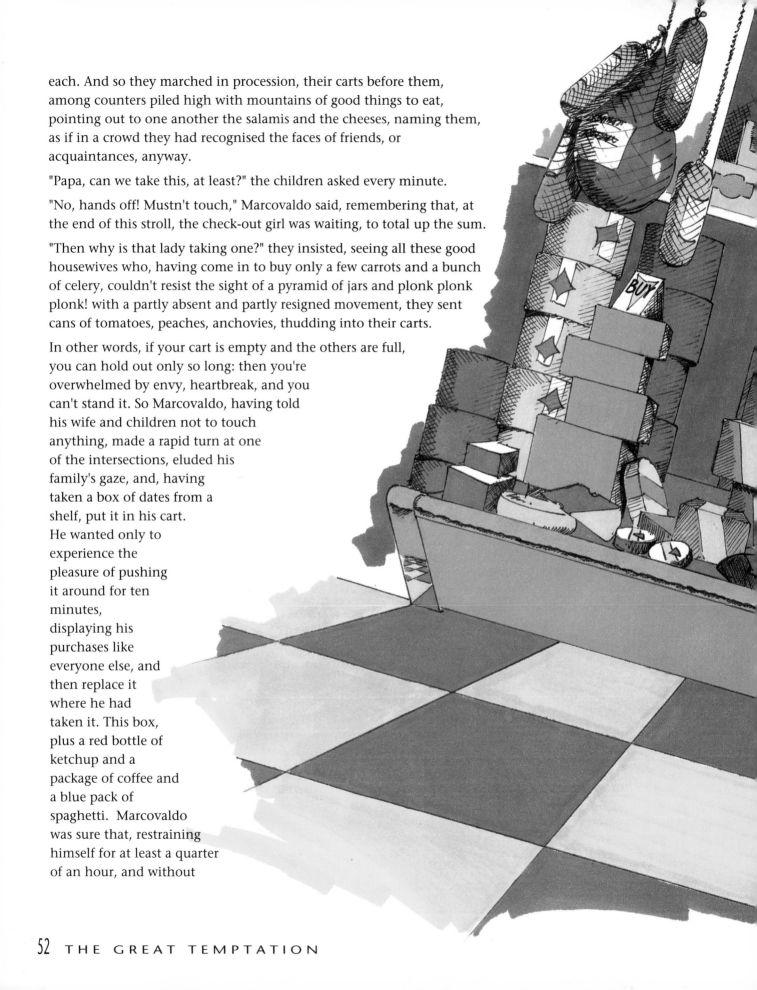

each. And so they marched in procession, their carts before them, among counters piled high with mountains of good things to eat, pointing out to one another the salamis and the cheeses, naming them, as if in a crowd they had recognised the faces of friends, or acquaintances, anyway.

"Papa, can we take this, at least?" the children asked every minute.

"No, hands off! Mustn't touch," Marcovaldo said, remembering that, at the end of this stroll, the check-out girl was waiting, to total up the sum.

"Then why is that lady taking one?" they insisted, seeing all these good housewives who, having come in to buy only a few carrots and a bunch of celery, couldn't resist the sight of a pyramid of jars and plonk plonk plonk! with a partly absent and partly resigned movement, they sent cans of tomatoes, peaches, anchovies, thudding into their carts.

In other words, if your cart is empty and the others are full, you can hold out only so long: then you're overwhelmed by envy, heartbreak, and you can't stand it. So Marcovaldo, having told his wife and children not to touch anything, made a rapid turn at one of the intersections, eluded his family's gaze, and, having taken a box of dates from a shelf, put it in his cart. He wanted only to experience the pleasure of pushing it around for ten minutes, displaying his purchases like everyone else, and then replace it where he had taken it. This box, plus a red bottle of ketchup and a package of coffee and a blue pack of spaghetti. Marcovaldo was sure that, restraining himself for at least a quarter of an hour, and without

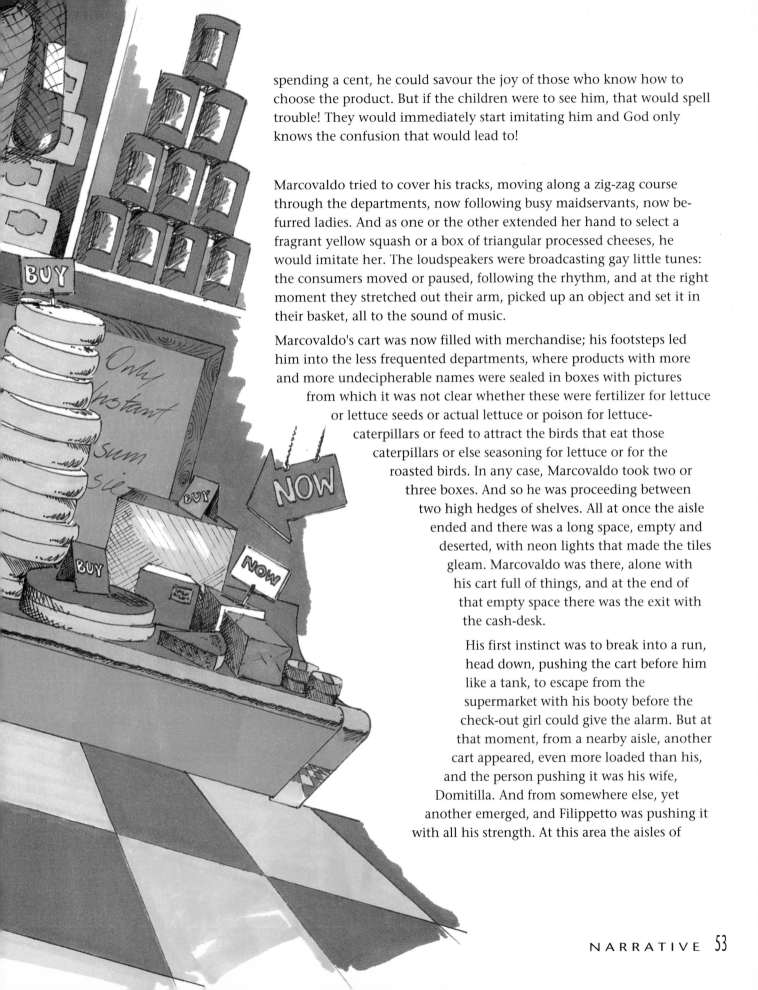

spending a cent, he could savour the joy of those who know how to choose the product. But if the children were to see him, that would spell trouble! They would immediately start imitating him and God only knows the confusion that would lead to!

Marcovaldo tried to cover his tracks, moving along a zig-zag course through the departments, now following busy maidservants, now be-furred ladies. And as one or the other extended her hand to select a fragrant yellow squash or a box of triangular processed cheeses, he would imitate her. The loudspeakers were broadcasting gay little tunes: the consumers moved or paused, following the rhythm, and at the right moment they stretched out their arm, picked up an object and set it in their basket, all to the sound of music.

Marcovaldo's cart was now filled with merchandise; his footsteps led him into the less frequented departments, where products with more and more undecipherable names were sealed in boxes with pictures from which it was not clear whether these were fertilizer for lettuce or lettuce seeds or actual lettuce or poison for lettuce-caterpillars or feed to attract the birds that eat those caterpillars or else seasoning for lettuce or for the roasted birds. In any case, Marcovaldo took two or three boxes. And so he was proceeding between two high hedges of shelves. All at once the aisle ended and there was a long space, empty and deserted, with neon lights that made the tiles gleam. Marcovaldo was there, alone with his cart full of things, and at the end of that empty space there was the exit with the cash-desk.

His first instinct was to break into a run, head down, pushing the cart before him like a tank, to escape from the supermarket with his booty before the check-out girl could give the alarm. But at that moment, from a nearby aisle, another cart appeared, even more loaded than his, and the person pushing it was his wife, Domitilla. And from somewhere else, yet another emerged, and Filippetto was pushing it with all his strength. At this area the aisles of

many departments converged, and from each opening one of the Marcovaldo's children appeared, all pushing carts laden like freighters. Each had had the same idea, and now, meeting, they realised they had assembled a complete sampling of all the supermarket's possibilities. "Papa, are we rich then?" Michelino asked. "Will we have food to eat for a year?"

"Go back! Hurry! Get away from that desk!" Marcovaldo cried, doing an about-face and hiding, himself and his victuals, behind the counters; and he began to dash, bent double as if under enemy fire, to become lost once more among the various departments. A rumble resounded behind him; he turned and saw the whole family, galloping at his heels, pushing their carts in line, like a train.

"They'll charge us a million for this!"

The supermarket was large and complex as a labyrinth: you could roam around it for hours and hours. With all these provisions at their disposal, Marcovaldo and family could have spent the winter there, never coming out. But the loudspeakers had already stopped their tunes, and were saying: "Attention, please! In fifteen minutes the supermarket will close! Please proceed to the check-out counters!"

It was time to get rid of their cargo: now or never. At the summons of the loudspeaker, the crowd of customers was gripped by a frantic haste, as if these were the last minutes in the last supermarket of the whole world, an urgency either to grab everything there was or to leave it there - the motive wasn't clear - and there was a pushing and shoving around all the shelves. Marcovaldo, Domitilla and the children took advantage of it to replace goods on the counters or to slip things into other people's carts. The replacements were somewhat random: the flypaper ended on the ham shelf, a cabbage landed among the cakes. They didn't realise that, instead of a cart, one lady was pushing a baby carriage with an infant inside; they stuck a bottle of Barbera in with it.

Depriving themselves of things like this, without even having tasted them, was a torment that brought tears to the eyes. And so, at the very moment they abandoned a jar of mayonnaise, they came upon a bunch of bananas, and took it; or a roast chicken to substitute for a nylon broom; with this system the more they emptied their carts, the more they filled them.

The family with their provisions went up and down the escalators, and at every level, on all sides they found themselves facing obligatory routes that led to a check-out cashier, who aimed an adding machine, chattering like a machine gun, at all those who showed signs of leaving. The wandering of Marcovaldo and family resembled more and more that of caged animals or of prisoners in a luminous prison with walls of coloured panels.

In one place, the panels of one wall had been dismantled; there was a ladder set there, hammers, carpenter's and mason's tools. A contractor was building an annexe to the supermarket. Their working day over, the men had gone off, leaving everything where it was. Marcovaldo, his provisions before him, passed through the hole in the wall. Ahead there was darkness: he advanced. And his family, with their carts, came after him.

The rubber wheels of the carts jolted over the ground, sandy at times, as if cobbles had been removed, then on a floor of loose planks. Marcovaldo proceeded, poised, along a plank; the others followed him. All of a sudden they saw, before and behind, above and below, many lights strewn in the darkness, and all around, the void.

They were on the wooden structure of a scaffolding, at the level of seven-storey houses. The city opened below them in a luminous sparkle of windows and signs and the electric spray from tram antennae; higher up, the

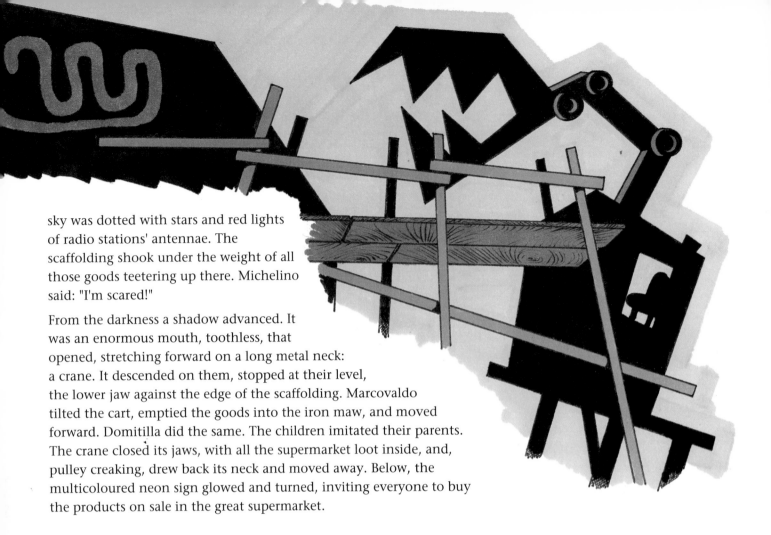

sky was dotted with stars and red lights of radio stations' antennae. The scaffolding shook under the weight of all those goods teetering up there. Michelino said: "I'm scared!"

From the darkness a shadow advanced. It was an enormous mouth, toothless, that opened, stretching forward on a long metal neck: a crane. It descended on them, stopped at their level, the lower jaw against the edge of the scaffolding. Marcovaldo tilted the cart, emptied the goods into the iron maw, and moved forward. Domitilla did the same. The children imitated their parents. The crane closed its jaws, with all the supermarket loot inside, and, pulley creaking, drew back its neck and moved away. Below, the multicoloured neon sign glowed and turned, inviting everyone to buy the products on sale in the great supermarket.

Reading the story

1 Do you think this story sets out to give you an attractive picture of shopping? Give reasons for your answer.

2 How would you describe Marcovaldo and his family? Place the following statements about them in order of importance and add at least one statement of your own:
   • they are poor
   • they are unsure how to behave
   • they are people who long for the things that money can buy
   • they are dreamers
   • they are disorganised.

3 Why do you think that Italo Calvino has chosen to tell this story? Choose one of these four suggestions or decide on your own reason:

   • He wrote it because he hates supermarkets.
   • He wrote it because he is addicted to supermarkets.
   • He wrote it because he felt sorry for people like Marcovaldo.
   • He wrote it to make fun of the way human beings behave.
   Explain your decision.

4 What picture has formed in your head of the supermarket? Choose three or four short quotations from the story that best describe the supermarket.

5 Do you think this story is set in the past, the present or the future? Give reasons for your view.

From one writer to another

Reading a story can be the starting point for your own writing. This does not mean copying the story, but making one of its ideas work for you.

Write your own piece set in a supermarket. This could be a story, a monologue or a short play.

Do not worry about a complicated plot, but concentrate on getting all the atmosphere of the place. The following ideas will give you a starter:

- the assistants who are supposed to help and don't know where anything is because they started last week and only work afternoons

- the snippets of conversations that you catch between couples or families as they go around

- the numbered ticket system for some counters where your number is never called unless you are elsewhere so you never get a turn

- uncontrolled seven-year-olds who think the supermarket is a giant play zone for war games

- the fact that whichever checkout queue you join is always the slowest because the person at the front has bought a yogurt which has to be replaced by the supervisor because it has a hole in it

- the person who tries to pay by cheque and finds that they haven't got a cheque card, nor any identification nor any cash

- the realisation, as you head back to the car park, that you have forgotten the one item that you came for in the first place.

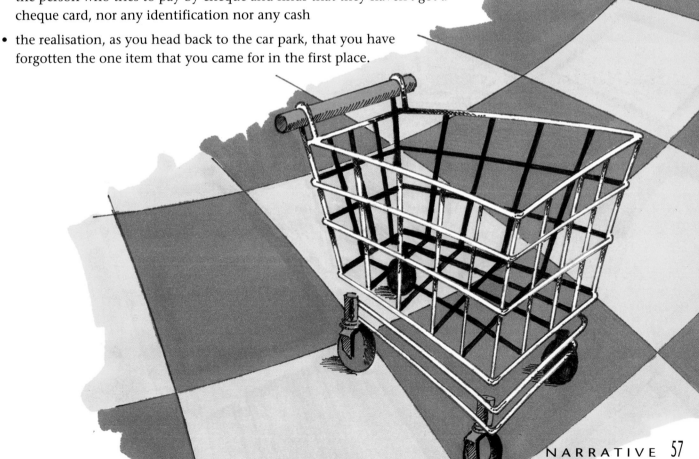

HONEST
I WOULD

What would *you* do if you were in an awkward situation? Not what do you think you *ought* to do but what would you *actually* do? And can the rest of your group guess what you would do? In each round of this game, one person is the *silent one* and the rest of the group has to guess what he or she has written.

THE RULES

- Arrange yourselves in a circle or a square.

- Decide who will be the *silent one*.

- Listen as the teacher calls the number of the situation for the first round.

- Each member of the group writes down what they would do...truthfully!

- The *silent one* hides his/her answer.

- The other members of the group read out their own answers and guess what the *silent one* has written.

- The *silent one* finishes off the round by reading out his/her views and saying who was closest to guessing them.

- The *silent one* then chooses a number for the person on their right and the process is repeated.

- The game continues until the situations have all been used up or the time allowed runs out.

The situations

1 Your friend has lent you their CD player whilst they are on holiday and, whilst it still works, one of the programming functions seems to have got broken, probably because you dropped the remote control...

2 You see a policeman having problems arresting an unarmed man...

3 You are offered a job in a shop on Saturdays but the owner tells you that it's strictly unofficial and cash in hand...

4 You know that two members of your class are using material originally written by their brighter older brother/sister for an assignment that is being counted towards their final examination grade...

5 You find an expensive pen left in a telephone box...

6 Your friend picks his or her nose in public and is quite unaware of the fact...

7 Your parents agree to go out whilst you have a party so long as it is alcohol-free. When your friends are told about this they start planning how to "help" you by smuggling in booze...

8 You stumble across your best friend's private diary...

9 You see a member of your class taking money from a teacher's unattended bag. You are the only person who sees it...

10 Your next door neighbours have left the keys to the house so that you can feed the budgie. They also have a magnificent collection of tapes and CDs that they guard jealously...

11 You have a boyfriend/girlfriend and his/her family have invited you to go on holiday with them. Your parents are, to put it mildly, not amused...

12 A friend sometimes shoplifts when you are with them and has come close to getting caught...

13 The school is having a 24 hour sponsored event. Your parents are not sure whether to allow you to take part...

14 A boy has recently arrived in your class from Singapore. You do not know whether it is because he is bright or because he is a slightly different colour or because he is new but, for some reason, he is getting a lot of verbal abuse. You know he is getting very upset by it but he says nothing...

15 A friend borrows some of your GCSE homework and does a straight copy. You are now both in trouble...

Writing

Use one of these situations as a starting point for a story of your own. Change the details as necessary to create a convincing tale.

THE POETS SAY...

...well what *do* they say? Can you ever be sure? Is every person's opinion equally valid? Do some reactions to a poem make more sense than others?

This section gives you two poems on a similar subject to look at with these questions in mind.

What does the poem say?

Read **Promises Like Pie-Crust** opposite and then discuss the following questions in your groups.

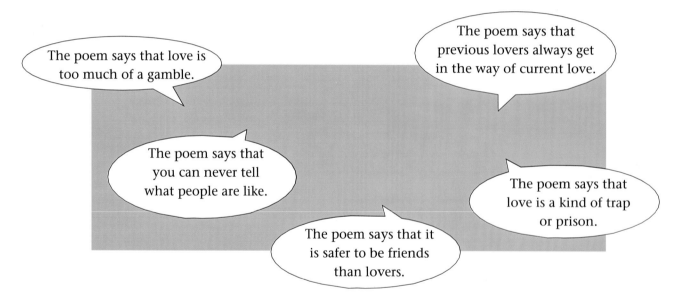

> The poem says that love is too much of a gamble.

> The poem says that previous lovers always get in the way of current love.

> The poem says that you can never tell what people are like.

> The poem says that love is a kind of trap or prison.

> The poem says that it is safer to be friends than lovers.

What evidence can you find in the poem for these statements?
Which statement sums up the poem best of all? Why?
How would you finish the following two statements?

> The poem says that promises are like pie-crust because...

> The poem's main message is...

Promises Like Pie-Crust

Promise me no promises,
So will I not promise you:
Keep we both our liberties,
Never false and never true:
Let us hold the die uncast,
Free to come as free to go:
For I cannot know your past,
And of mine what can you know?

You, so warm, may once have been
Warmer towards another one:
I, so cold, may once have seen
Sunlight, once have felt the sun:
Who shall show us if it was
Thus indeed in time of old?
Fades the image from the glass,
And the fortune is not told.

If you promised, you might grieve
For lost liberty again:
If I promised, I believe
I should fret to break the chain.
Let us be the friends we were,
Nothing more but nothing less:
Many thrive on frugal fare
Who would perish of excess.

Christina Rossetti

Kahlil Gibran wrote at a different time and in a different place from Christina Rossetti, but they shared at least some of the same concerns. This is an extract from his book **The Prophet**. Read it, then tackle the *Responses* section which follows.

Love one another, but make not a bond of love:
Let it rather be a moving sea between the shores of your souls.
Fill each other's cup but drink not from one cup.
Give one another of your bread but eat not from the same loaf.
Sing and dance together and be joyous, but let each one of you be alone,
Even as the strings of a lute are alone though they quiver with the same music.
Give your hearts, but not into each other's keeping.

For only the hand of Life can contain your hearts.
And stand together yet not too near together:
For the pillars of the temple stand apart,
And the oak tree and the cypress grow not in each other's shadow.

Kahlil Gibran

Responses

Complete these responses to the poem.

The poem says that...
(Try to come up with three or four statements.)

The poem is similar to Promises Like Pie-Crust because...

The poem is different because...

Options for writing

1 Write up the ideas from your discussion about the attitudes to love shown by these writers.

2 Look at other love poems and make the two you have studied here the start of a wider survey of love poetry.

GETTING
THE RIGHT IDEA

An important difference between most poems and a novel or a play is the size. A poem is often trying to tell a story or describe a scene in only a page or two. Look at what Fleur Adcock has managed to do in less than fifty lines.

The telephone call

They asked me "Are you sitting down?
Right? This is Universal Lotteries"
they said. "You've won the top prize,
the Ultra-super Global Special.
What would you do with a million pounds?
Or, actually, with more than a million –
not that it makes a lot of difference
once you're a millionaire." And they laughed.

"Are you OK?" they asked – "Still there?
Come on, now, tell us, how does it feel?"
I said "I just...I can't believe it!"
They said "That's what they all say.
What else? Go on, tell us about it."
I said "I feel the top of my head
has floated off, out through the window,
revolving like a flying saucer."

"That's unusual" they said. "Go on."
I said "I'm finding it hard to talk.
My throat's gone dry, my nose is tingling.
I think I'm going to sneeze – or cry."
"That's right" they said, "don't be ashamed
of giving way to your emotions.
It isn't every day you hear
you're going to get a million pounds.

Relax now, have a little cry;
we'll give you a moment..." "Hang on!" I said.
"I haven't bought a lottery ticket
for years and years. And what did you say
the company's called?" They laughed again.
"Not to worry about a ticket.
We're Universal. We operate
a Retrospective Chances Module.

Nearly everyone's bought a ticket
in some lottery or another,
once at least. We buy up the files,
feed the names into our computer,
and see who the lucky person is."
"Well, that's incredible" I said.
"It's marvellous. I still can't quite...
I'll believe it when I see the cheque."

"Oh," they said, "there's no cheque."
"But the money?" "We don't deal in money.
Experiences are what we deal in.
You've had a great experience, right?
Exciting? Something you'll remember?
That's your prize. So congratulations
from all of us at Universal.
Have a nice day!" And the phone went dead.

Fleur Adcock

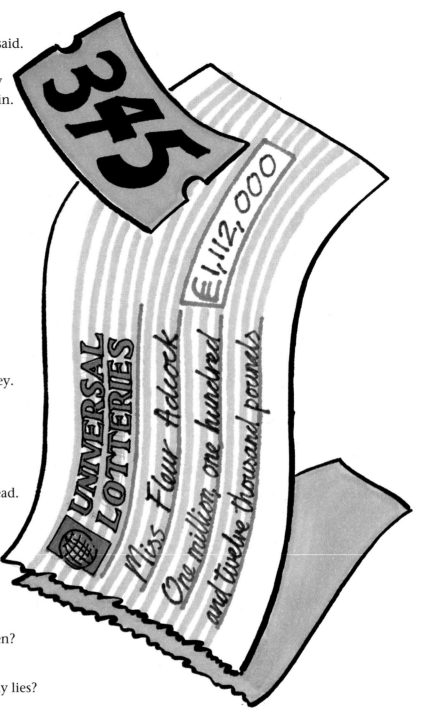

First reactions

1 Did you guess what was going to happen?

2 If you did, what gave you a clue?

3 Did the telephone caller actually tell any lies?

The poem manages to squeeze a smile out of most people.

• What do you think makes most people smile or laugh
  when they read or hear it?

• Which are your favourite lines or phrases?

• What do you like about them?

The right idea

How on earth do people think up ideas like the one in **The Telephone Call?** This is part of what Fleur Adcock had to say about the poem:

"The idea came to me as I was lying in the bath one morning, thinking of how the telephone always tends to ring when I'm in the bath, and how it's seldom anything worth rushing out, dripping wet, to answer. But what would be worth getting out of the bath for?"

What telephone call would you be more than happy to receive? What knock on the front door might transform your world? By following the thought routes below, see what ideas you can develop yourself and turn one of them into a story or poem of your own.

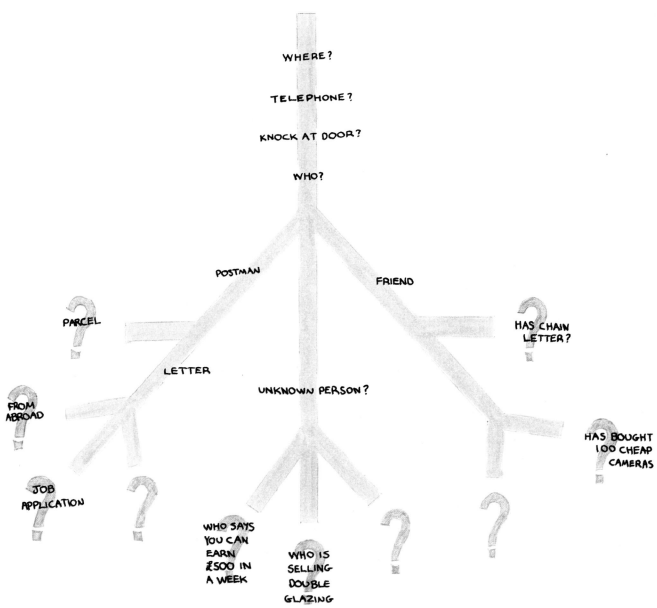

WHAT ON EARTH CAN I SAY?

If you are asked to talk or write about a story, there are usually some obvious places to start: a character's attitude or a surprise twist in the plot. It is not always as clear where to start with a poem, which is much more compact.

Look at the following poem in which the Welsh writer, Tony Curtis, remembers a story he heard:

STRONGMAN

A strongman you say.
Home from work would stretch his arms
and hang his five sons from them
turning like a roundabout.
A carpenter who could punch nails
into wood with a clenched fist,
chest like a barrel with a neck
that was like holding onto a tree.

In the final hour
your hands between the sheets
to lift him to the lavatory
slipped under a frame of bones like plywood.
No trouble - he said. No trouble, Dad -
you said. And he died in the cradle of your arms.

Tony Curtis

First reactions

• distress at the effect of the illness?

• a sense of shock at the change in the older man?

• our helplessness when faced with some diseases?

Put your own feelings into a sentence or two.
Pick a line or phrase from the poem that struck home
to you.

Well, what is there to discuss or think about?

Details

Title
Why did he call it **Strongman?**

Verses
Why did he divide the poem in two like that?

Contrasts
For example, youth and age - looking at the
difference time has made to the father.

Words and phrases
How do the ones which struck you help to give a
picture of what is happening?

Meaning
What does the poem say to you? Many poems can
be seen in several ways depending on what a
reader has selected as important.

What about when they give you more than one poem?

That makes the work easier because with two or more
poems you have something to compare. Look at the
following poem by Elma Mitchell.

It's Mother, You See

It's mother you see.
I cannot fold her up like a pram or a bicycle.
It's every day crawling around the agencies.
I cannot leave her alone in a furnished room.
She has to come with me, arm in arm, umbrella'd,
Or trailing a little.

She is thin in wind and limb,
She is not quite white in the head,
Now and then she stops – suddenly and completely
Like a mutinous dog on a lead.

(And once, long ago, in reverse,
I trailed after her skirts in the thronging streets,
Her basket of goodies
Bobbing just out of my reach.)

She's no need to stare at the shops.
We have plenty more clothes, if we bothered to open the cases,
And hundreds of photographs of the way things were.
Sometimes we take out a bit of the better china
And wash it and put it away again.

It is every day to the agents,
Then on to the library, checking the papers for ads.
Or walking the streets looking for signs that might say
Where to apply for a key.

It is hard on the legs, it is hard on the wits and the heart,
But I cannot leave her alone in a furnished room.
O come on, Mum. One day we'll find us a home
Somewhere this side of the sky.

Elma Mitchell

First reactions

All right, we've read it. Now what do we do?

• did you respond to the humour?

• did the situation make you sad?

• does the poem arouse your sympathy?

Put your own feelings into a few words.
Choose a line or phrase from the poem that struck home to you.

Details

Title
What does the title make you think about the
poet's mother?

Verse
Often you will find that different verses deal with
different aspects of a poem.

Contrasts
You could look at the differences between what
they have and what they need.

Words and phrases
What do they mean? What pictures / images do
they leave in your mind?

Meaning
In what way might Elma Mitchell be wanting to
influence the reader's views through this poem?

Comparisons

What does this poem share with the poem by Tony Curtis?
In what ways are they different?

Is that it?

Not exactly. There are nearly always new things
waiting to be discovered in a poem but you now
have the basis for writing about your response to the
poems.

TAKING YOUR SENSES FOR A WALK

High Street Smells

A busy street is a public library of smells –
the coffee grinder's fresh aroma at the corner,
the baker's sweet, buttery perfume –
you can almost taste the rolls, the pasties,
and drink the toasted coffee on the morning air.

Out of the sweet shops and the candy stores
oozes the exotic scent of marzipan and chocolate,
and the plebeian breath of chewing gum and gobstoppers.
The fruit market is a pungent orchard of essential juices,
and my ever-wary nose tells me that I'm approaching
the butcher's, with its plain whiffs of blood and sawdust,
while the sea itself comes swimming right across the pavement
as I pass the fishmonger's briny bouquets in ice and salt.

The Chinese takeaway, the Indian curry restaurant,
the fish-and-chip shop, McDonald's (smell is flavour),
the Olde Worlde Teashoppe, all have their distinctive auras
and tangs of sweet and sour, poppedoms and spice,
deep-frying oil with vinegar. And toast, cakes and tea.

A gush of ironing steam from the laundry. The dry cleaner's
sharp, stinging reek, like smelling-salts – what a pong!

The pubs are open books of beer, wines and spirits
that my nostrils read rapidly, a kind of boozy braille.
The shoe emporium's rich emanations of supple leather, new shoes
impregnating the shoe boxes' pure white cardboard and tissue paper.
And here's the newsagent's – you can almost read the acrid print
of the local weekly, "The Farming World," "The People's Friend,"
"Popular Gardening", and all the comics before you even open them!
The voluptuous tobacconist's censes with its musky leaf
an entire shopping-mall – the drums, cartons and boxes
of honey shag, and tins of teasing snuff.

These are just some of the olfactory treats
for the aware nostril, the adventurous nose
seeking, among the banal stink and stench of exhaust fumes
the characters, the eccentrics, the silent friends
that are the original fragrances of busy streets.

James Kirkup

Residence in London

And first the look and aspect of the place
The broad high-way appearance, as it strikes
On Strangers of all ages, the quick dance
Of colours, lights and forms, the Babel din
The endless stream of men, and moving things,
From hour to hour the illimitable walk
Still among streets with clouds and sky above,
The wealth, the bustle and the eagerness,
The glittering Chariots with their pamper'd Steeds,
Stalls, Barrows, Porters; midway in the Street
The Scavenger, who begs with hat in hand,

The labouring Hackney Coaches, the rash speed
Of Coaches travelling far, whirl'd on with horn
Loud blowing, and the sturdy Drayman's Team,
Ascending from some Alley of the Thames
And striking right across the crowded Strand
Till the fore Horse veers round with punctual skill:
Here there and everywhere a weary throng
The Comers and the Goers face to face,
Face after face; the string of dazzling Wares,
Shop after shop, with Symbols, Blazon'd Names,
And all the Tradesman's honours overhead;

William Wordsworth

Taking your senses for a walk

"How extraordinary ordinary things are...like the process of observing."

These two poems are about the process of observing and experiencing. They are both set in cities. One is the London of the late eighteenth century. The other could be set in any British city in the late twentieth century.

1 Read them aloud in small groups until you are happy with the way they sound.

2 **High Street Smells** concentrates on smells. How many senses are described in the extract from Wordsworth? Which senses are most important in the poem? How are they described?

3 How well has the writer of **High Street Smells** captured the feel of city streets?

4 Reconstruct the eighteenth century street scene in **Residence in London** as a piece of prose descriptive writing. The illustration will help you start.

Looking at language

1 Look closely at *Residence in London*. Are there any words which we no longer use? Find out what they mean.

2 What other differences can you see between Wordsworth's language and the English we speak and write today?

3 Both poems use powerful imagery, especially metaphors (when something is described as if it were literally something else). For example, "A busy street is a public library of smells" and "the quick dance of colours".

Select three powerful uses of imagery from each poem, giving the reasons for your selection.

> **HELP**
>
> For extra help with literary terms see the glossary in the **Heinemann English Assessment and Reference File** on pages 61 to 63.

Street scenes

Using a similar technique, take your senses for a walk along two very different streets. The contrast could be that of place – country and city; season – winter and summer, or time – Friday night and Sunday morning. It could even be that of history – then and now.

Whichever you choose, imagine yourself in the very centre of your chosen streets. Look up, look down, look behind you, don't hide in the shadows.

Describe the extraordinary, everyday things you experience as two contrasting poems.

THE BALLAD OF SPRINGHILL

The Springhill Mine Disaster

In the town of Springhill, Nova Scotia,
Down in the dark of the Cumberland Mine,
There's blood on the coal and the miners lie
In the roads that never saw sun nor sky.

In the town of Springhill, you don't sleep easy,
Often the earth will tremble and roll,
When the earth is restless, miners die,
Bone and blood is the price of coal.

In the town of Springhill, Nova Scotia,
Late in the year of fifty-eight,
Day still comes and the sun still shines,
But it's dark as the grave in the Cumberland Mine.

Down at the coal face, miners working
Rattle of the belt and the cutter's blade,
Rumble of rock and the walls close round
The living and the dead men two miles down.

Twelve men lay two miles from the pitshaft,
Twelve men lay in the dark and sang,
Long, hot days in the miner's tomb,
It was three feet high and a hundred long.

Three days passed and the lamps gave out,
And Caleb Rushton he up and said:
"There's no more water nor light nor bread
So we'll live on songs and hope instead."

Listen for the shouts of the bareface miners,
Listen through the rubble for a rescue team,
Six-hundred feet of coal and slag,
Hope imprisoned in a three-foot seam.

Eight days passed and some were rescued,
Leaving the dead to lie alone
Through all their lives they dug a grave,
Two miles of earth for a marking stone.

Ewan MacColl & Peggy Seeger

First reactions

1 What do you think is the most tragic aspect of the mining disaster?

2 Which lines bring out the tragedy most effectively for you?

Group Performance

Ballads are normally written to be sung or spoken aloud. Prepare a reading of this poem for three or four voices. You will need to decide who reads which lines and how they read them. Think about:

- the way that the poem is broken into verses

- the way the verses divide into parts or have clear contrasts of mood or action that can be brought out by using different voices

- making the story clear for your audience

- how you want your audience to feel about the disaster.

Ballad to newspaper report

There is a great difference between the way this ballad tells the story of the disaster and the way a newspaper would report it. Below are headlines and reports which some of today's newspapers might have carried after the tragedy.

Mine Disaster

Full report page 7

More than a dozen men are feared trapped by the collapse of at least one shaft at the Cumberland Mine yesterday. Reports are still not clear as to the extent of the

THREE FOOT HELL

"Absolutely no chance" says rescue leader

Hope is fading for the miners trapped by the collapse of the main shaft in the Cumberland Mine last Thursday. After 72 hours of non-stop work the rescue brigade are not even at the

GOT 'EM

Rescue magic means miracle escape for some

"We've got em" was the message Jack Butterworth yelled at his mates on the rescue team.

And they had. The lads had broken through over 600 feet

Which newspaper?

1 Newspapers write their articles in very different styles. In which newspaper might you find each of the three extracts?

2 What do you think might attract readers to each of these styles?

The facts

A good journalist will want to make sure that the facts are reported accurately.

Looking back at the poem, sort out what you see as the facts in this case, and note them down.

Writing the article

A newspaper report tells you more than what happened. It also gives the views and feelings of people who were involved in the incident. The people a journalist might interview in this situation include relatives of miners who died, local politicians, the mine owners or managers, members of the rescue team and a member of the committee responsible for safety in mines.

A journalist's report is never written from the account of one person. What people say may be influenced, for example, by grief, by their social position or by how they think their job might be affected. Newspaper articles can be radically different depending on whose views are reported in them.

Either:

Finish one of the newspaper reports on the Cumberland Mine on the opposite page.

or:

Write your own report on the Cumberland Mine disaster for a paper of your choice. Include interviews with people involved in the incident - some of them and what they might say are shown below.

> **HELP**
> For a reminder about the layout and style of newspaper articles, look at pages 158 and 159. There is further guidance on writing for newspapers in **Heinemann English Assessment and Reference File,** pages 80 and 81.

We worked around the clock. You can't do more than that, can you?

Member of rescue team

I have made arrangements for the setting up of a disaster fund and, from tomorrow, people will be able to make donations at every local bank.

Mayoress

Our company has done all it can throughout to assist the rescuers.

Pit manager

I don't know who's to blame, but somebody ought to come and explain to my kids why they've got no daddy. I can't.

Wife of dead miner

MORE THAN JUST WORDS ON A PAGE

The dialogue and stage directions of a play have to be interpreted and brought to life for performance. The first part of the following short play has been annotated with some of the questions that one group asked when they were preparing it for performance. They decided on the answers to their questions either by acting out an idea or by discussing it. With your group, do the same for the second part of the play.

REQUEST STOP

why small?
what sort of raincoat?
- what impression should he give

A queue at a Request Bus Stop. A WOMAN *at the head, with a* SMALL MAN *in a raincoat next to her, two other* WOMEN *and a* MAN.

NAMES - No one is given one. Why ??

WOMAN (*to* SMALL MAN) I beg your pardon, what did you say?

Pause.

what is the tone of this?
polite?
threatening?

what on earth do we do with all these pauses?

All I asked you was if I could get a bus from here to Shepherds Bush.

Pause.

Nobody asked you to start making insinuations.

Pause.

- how long are they?
- should she do anything in them?

Who do you think you are?

Pause.

Huh. I know your sort, I know your type. Don't worry, I know all about people like you.

Pause.

We can tell where you come from. They're putting your sort inside every day of the week.

how is the man reacting to all this?
is he ignoring it?

Pause.

how aggressive is she to be played?

All I've got to do, is report you, and you'd be standing in the dock in next to no time. One of my best friends is a plain clothes detective.

Pause.

how much is she a real threat and how much is she disconcerting but unhinged?

I know all about it. Standing there as if butter wouldn't melt in your mouth. Meet you in a dark alley it'd be.... another story. (*To the others, who stare into space*) You heard what this man said to me. All I asked him was if I could get a bus from here to Shepherds Bush. (*To him*) I've got witnesses, don't you worry about that.

The others don't want to know. How do you make it clear they're staring into space and not just standing there?

Pause.

Impertinence.

Pause.

Ask a man a civil question he treats you like a threepenny bit. *(To him)* I've got better things to do, my lad, I can assure you. I'm not going to stand here and be insulted on a public highway. Anyone can tell you're just up from the country for a bit of a lark. I know your sort.

Pause.

She goes to a LADY.

Excuse me lady. I'm thinking of taking this man up to the magistrate's court, you heard him make that crack, would you like to be a witness?

The LADY *steps into the road.*

LADY: Taxi...

She disappears.

WOMAN: We know what sort she is. *(Back to position)* I was the first in this queue.

Pause.

Born just round the corner. Born and bred. These people from the country haven't the faintest idea of how to behave. Peruvians. You're bloody lucky I don't put you on a charge. You ask a straightforward question -

The others suddenly thrust out their arms at a passing bus. They run off left after it. The WOMAN, *alone, clicks her teeth and mutters. A man walks from the right to the stop, and waits. She looks at him out of the corner of her eye. At length she speaks shyly, hesitantly, with a slight smile.*

Excuse me. Do you know if I can get a bus from here...to Marble Arch?

Harold Pinter

Different performances

If possible, watch several groups perform this scene. Listen to the discussion and the performances on the cassette.

1 What differences are there in interpretation?

2 Which parts work best in each production?

Queue for a play

A bus stop is not the only place you find a queue or some other group of
people who are waiting. Look at these possible settings for a short play
involving a group of waiting people:

cinema	airport
railway station	getting tickets for a rock concert
doctor's waiting room	dentist's
school canteen	hospital casualty
outside the headteacher's room	

Choose one of them and draft your own short scene.

You will find it helpful to limit yourself to only a few speaking
parts.

The following play openings written by three students will give you
ideas on how to approach the task.

"The flight now boarding..."

A smartly-dressed woman is sitting in the airport lounge waiting for her flight. A second woman enters.

FIRST WOMAN: Is this seat taken?

SECOND WOMAN: No, I suppose not.

FIRST WOMAN: What flight are you taking, love?

SECOND WOMAN: Concorde. How else would one fly?

FIRST WOMAN: Oh, well I'm taking a package holiday to Majorca. In fact my flight is due in about ten
minutes' time - right on time, just as scheduled. What time is your flight due?

SECOND WOMAN: Nearly three hours ago.

Fiona

"Open wide..."

A dentist's waiting room. An old lady is sitting next to a mother and her young son. A teenage girl is reading a magazine and a teenage boy is watching the girl and pretending to read a magazine.

OLD LADY: (*talking to mother*) I had my teeth until I was sixty and I had no problems. I've had these dentures five minutes and I've had no end of problems.

MOTHER: Oh, that's terrible. (*to son*) Johnny, stop that. Put it down where you found it.

JOHHNY: I want to go to the toilet mummy.

MOTHER: I thought you went before we left home.

JOHNNY: I did but I want to go again.

Heulwen

"I'll wait for the video, next time"

Outside a cinema. The queue appears to have been waiting a long time.

BOY: How much longer now mum?

MUM: Shouldn't be much longer now.

BOY: But we've been waiting for ages. I'm bored.

MUM: There's nothing I can do about it. Now why don't you play "I Spy" with Sophie?

BOY: I don't want to play with her. She cheats.

GIRL: No I don't.

BOY: Do.

GIRL: Don't.

BOY: Do.

MUM: Both of you, quiet. Billy, I'm sure Sophie doesn't cheat.

BOY: Yes she does. She uses words like "claustrophobic". How can you spy a claustrophobic?

GIRL: Just because you don't know what it means.

BOY: Yes I do.

GIRL: Don't.

BOY: Do.

GIRL: Don't.

MUM: (*almost shouting*) Be quiet! I don't care if you play "I Spy" or not but you can be quiet or we're going home right now.

Vici

WRITING FOR RADIO

INTRODUCTION

Radio works on the principle that anything which can be described can be imagined. A radio play can travel between centuries and continents. It can take place in the most exotic locations or within the thoughts of one person. However, this also means that radio has to attract and hold its audience using sound alone.

One way of doing this is to have interesting and exciting dialogue. But a writer also needs to consider sound effects, music and silence. Pauses at the end of scenes help listeners to digest what they have heard and prepare for what happens next.

This unit examines radio plays by looking at a well known serial, *The Archers*. Set in the imaginary village of Ambridge, the daily experiences of the Archer family and other villagers have captivated radio listeners for over forty years.

We will be looking first at how the episodes are planned and written. We will then look at some of the techniques used to make the characters, setting and plot realistic and three-dimensional using sound only.

THE STORY OF A STORYLINE

Episodes of **The Archers** are prepared some three months before transmission.

Firstly, a team of writers meets at a *script meeting*, together with various editors, researchers and producers. The script meeting will agree on a set of *storylines* to be spread over all the episodes for the next four weeks.

Each individual writer is then allocated a week, and is expected to produce a set of programme *synopses* (a scene-by-scene outline) for each of the five episodes in their particular week.

Once the synopses have been approved by the editor, the writer then produces *scripts* for each episode. Each episode usually consists of five scenes and must run for no more than the fifteen minutes allocated.

The scripts are then further modified, both at the read through on the day of recording and during recording itself, if the producer thinks it necessary.

Every character in **The Archers** has a detailed "biography" and these are used by the writers to ensure continuity.

HOW AN EPISODE IS MADE

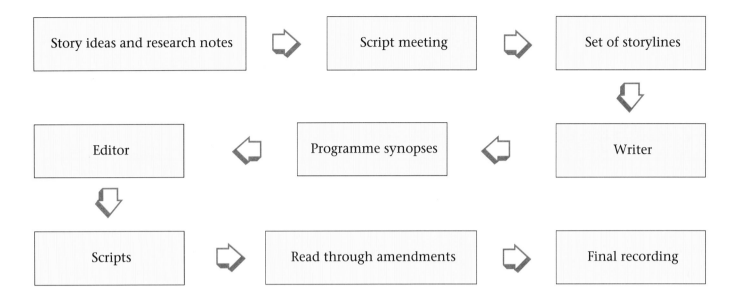

| Story ideas and research notes | ⇨ | Script meeting | ⇨ | Set of storylines |

```
Story ideas and research notes  ⇨  Script meeting  ⇨  Set of storylines
                                                              ⇩
        Editor  ⇦  Programme synopses  ⇦                    Writer
          ⇩
       Scripts  ⇨  Read through amendments  ⇨           Final recording
```

NOTES ON CHARACTERS

Phil Archer – Married to Jill Archer and they have four children: Kenton, Shula, David and Elizabeth. He runs Brookfield Farm in partnership with David.

Lynda Snell – Lives at Ambridge Hall with her husband Robert. Has two step children but they only visit for holidays. Enjoys rambling and organising village activities. Lynda will volunteer her services for any village activity often claiming exaggerated experience.

David Archer – Son of Phil and partner in Brookfield Farm. Married Ruth Pritchard in 1988 after a short romance. She has now finished Agricultural college and they have a home in a new bungalow built at Brookfield. He drives an XR3i and plays cricket for Ambridge and darts for The Bull.

Tom Forrest – Works part-time as a game keeper at Grey Gables, lives at Keeper's Cottage. He is a churchwarden and a bell-ringer at St Stephens.

George Barford – Works as the game keeper at Grey Gables and lives at The Stables with his wife Christine. Plays the cornet and is Chairman of the Parish Council.

CASE STUDY

The Montagu's Harriers

This particular storyline emerged from a set of detailed research notes prepared by the Agricultural Editor (Tony Parkin) and presented to a script meeting.

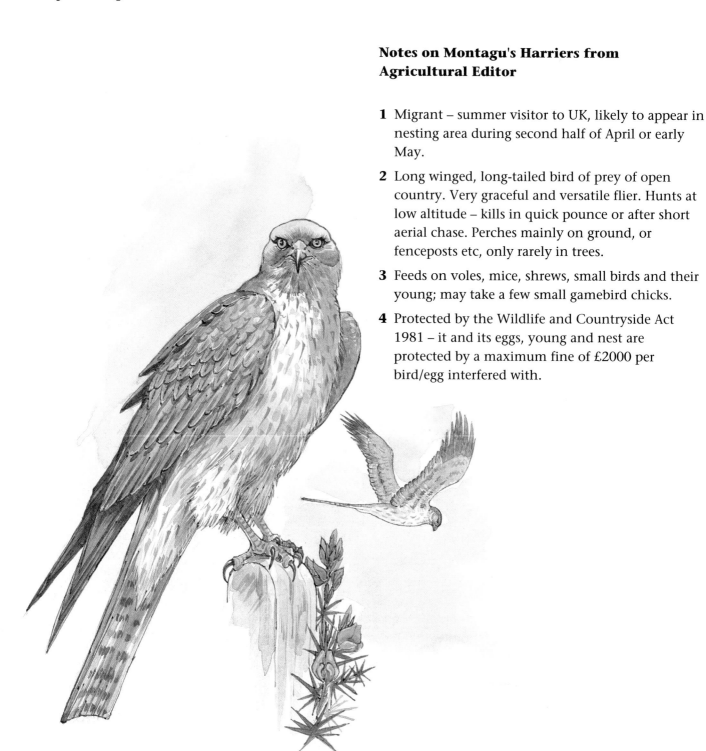

Notes on Montagu's Harriers from Agricultural Editor

1 Migrant – summer visitor to UK, likely to appear in nesting area during second half of April or early May.

2 Long winged, long-tailed bird of prey of open country. Very graceful and versatile flier. Hunts at low altitude – kills in quick pounce or after short aerial chase. Perches mainly on ground, or fenceposts etc, only rarely in trees.

3 Feeds on voles, mice, shrews, small birds and their young; may take a few small gamebird chicks.

4 Protected by the Wildlife and Countryside Act 1981 – it and its eggs, young and nest are protected by a maximum fine of £2000 per bird/egg interfered with.

THE SCRIPT MEETING

The script meeting accepts the general idea and suggests that it be used mainly as a story for Lynda Snell. It should begin during week three of the four-week cycle, continue into week four, and perhaps develop further from there.

Storyline notes from script meeting

(relevant to Harrier storyline)

Week Three

The Snells - Lynda's birthday. Last month Lynda gave Robert a wine cellar for his birthday. Eager to return the generosity Robert sets up a special party for Lynda. Maybe wine tasting will feature in the evening and Lynda gets a bit drunk. Going out for a walk the next day at Brookfield to clear her head she spots this peculiar bird - sizeable. The female is brown, speckled underneath with a 3ft wing span, has a long tail and is slightly slimmer than a buzzard. Is it a buzzard or could it be the extremely rare - Montagu's Harrier? She may also see the eggs, which would be laid on the ground in arable crops. After checking up in a book she realises it was indeed a Montagu's Harrier. Immediately warns Brookfield not to spray in the field, and sets up a vigil.

THE SYNOPSIS

The script writer concerned, Paul Burns, then inserts these suggestions into his synopsis for the relevant programme – Scenes Two and Four in Monday's episode.

Programme synopsis - Monday

Scene 2 Lynda, Tom
Exterior

Lynda is camped out in one of Phil's fields
watching the Montagu's Harrier. Tom has joined
her and confirms the rareness of her sighting.
He's never seen one round these parts. He
doesn't think George will be quite so enchanted
though – got to think of the pheasants. Lynda
asks Tom to keep it as quiet as he can. He'll do
his best but things like this have a way of
getting out.

Programme synopsis - Monday

Scene 4 Lynda, Phil, David
Exterior

On their way back from silage making, Phil and
David pass Lynda still on her lonely vigil (but
getting a bit impatient because Robert hasn't
come to relieve her yet). She bristles, expecting
another fight, but David wants to ask her about
the plastic bags.She says it's too late. They were
collected last week. There won't be another
collection for at least a month. She invites them
to look at the bird. Phil is quite impressed in
spite of himself but warns her against trampling
crops. She's being very, very careful about not
telling anyone.

THE FULL SCRIPT

Paul then writes the full script, incorporating
everything which has been agreed so far – the
agricultural notes, the storyline notes and the
programme synopsis, remembering to restrict the
action to the characters available.

The full script for *Scene Two* of Monday's programme follows:

SCENE 2. EXTERIOR. A BROOKFIELD FIELD. MORNING. LYNDA AND TOM ARE WATCHING THE MONTAGU'S HARRIER.

TOM	1	Is that him now?
LYNDA	2	Oh yes. Isn't he beautiful?
TOM	3	He's quite a sight all right. And there's a pair of them you say?
LYNDA	4	Oh yes. They've been building their nest all weekend.
TOM	5	Has she laid an egg yet?
LYNDA	6	I rather think she has. I haven't been able to get close enough to check. I don't want to disturb them.
TOM	7	No. Course not.
LYNDA	8	But she definitely hasn't left the nest this morning and he's been flying backwards and forwards with little treats for her.
TOM	9	Well, if I didn't know better I'd say he was a buzzard, but he can't be. They don't nest on the ground.
LYNDA	10	Just what I thought. So I looked it up in my new bird book. And there they were...Montagu's Harriers.
TOM	11	Are you sure about that?
LYNDA	12	Oh yes. I wasn't at first. It seemed so unlikely. So I 'phoned the RSPB and they sent charming young men down to have a look.
TOM	13	That'll be the two lads who were in the Bull on Friday will it?
LYNDA	14	Probably. Anyway, now it's official, Ambridge has its very own pair of Montagu's Harriers.
TOM	15	Well, well.
LYNDA	16	Why don't you take a look through my field glasses Mr Forrest?
TOM	17	(*taking them*) Thanks very much.
LYNDA	18	Can you see under the wings? The black tips and the pattern of dots? They're slimmer than a buzzard.
TOM	19	Oh aar. I've never seen markings quite like that before and I reckon I know most of the birds round these parts pretty well.
LYNDA	20	Apparently it's very unusual to spot one this far west.
TOM	21	Is that right? I wonder what brought them here?
LYNDA	22	That we'll probably never know.
TOM	23	Have you told Phil about this?
LYNDA	24	Oh yes. I didn't want him trampling over the eggs or spraying them. They're protected birds you know.
TOM	25	Mebbe so. But it must be a bit of a nuisance having them nest in the middle of your crop.
LYNDA	26	I suppose it does cause a slight amount of inconvenience, as I told Mr Archer, but we have to learn to get our priorities right.

TOM	27	Phil didn't mind then?
LYNDA	28	Not when I explained the importance of the event to him. Mr Archer's a very reasonable man. Unlike his son.
TOM	29	David have a go at you did he?
LYNDA	30	I'd rather not think about it if you don't mind Mr Forrest. He was really quite abusive. It almost brought on one of my migraines.
TOM	31	He can be a bit hot headed can David. But he don't mean anything by it. And if Phil agreed to leave the site alone...
LYNDA	32	Oh he did...
TOM	33	Then you'll have nothing to worry about from Brookfield. I'd watch out for George Barford though if I were you.
LYNDA	34	George Barford! What's it got to do with him?
TOM	35	He's got pheasant chicks just hatched over at Grey Gables. A bird like this can cause a lot of damage.
LYNDA	36	Oh but my Montagu's Harriers wouldn't hurt his chicks.
TOM	37	They're birds of prey aren't they?
LYNDA	38	Well, yes but...
TOM	39	And if I'm not mistaken that fellow's got something in his beak right now.
LYNDA	40	What? Let me have a look. Oh, that's not a chick. It's a mouse or a shrew.

TOM	41	This time mebbe.
LYNDA	42	I can assure you Mr Forrest, these birds are known to feed on mice and other small animals...
TOM	43	Never birds?
LYNDA	44	Well, yes they do hunt the occasional small bird.
TOM	45	I see.
LYNDA	46	But my contacts at the RSPB are adamant they don't pose a serious threat to game birds.
TOM	47	Well I hope you can convince George of that. And Brian Aldridge. Especially now he's got the Brookfield shooting.
LYNDA	48	I was rather hoping Mr Aldridge and Mr Barford wouldn't find out about the Harriers.
TOM	49	You mean you want to keep it a secret?
LYNDA	50	As far as possible. For the sake of the eggs, Mr Forrest. It would be a real tragedy if they weren't allowed to hatch out
TOM	51	Well, I agree with you there, Mrs Snell and, of course I won't breathe a word.
LYNDA	52	Thank you.
TOM	53	But I'm afraid news like this has a way of getting out whether we want it to or not.

Pause and reflect

1 Identify the points where the writer is using the research material provided for him.

2 Pick out the moments when the characters say and do things which suggest new story directions and possibilities.

3 In pairs, read through the script again, but read it as if you were recording it for radio.
- Which words would you emphasise? Where would you pause?
- When would you raise or lower your voice?
- What accent would you give each character?
- What sound effects, if any, would you use?

4  Listen to the studio recording of the same scene on the cassette. Compare this with your reading. Do they interpret it differently in any way?

5 From what you have heard of the characters in the scene, complete a full character "biography" for both Lynda Snell and Tom Forrest. To the information already given add your estimates of their likely ages, backgrounds, personalities, home life and wider interests. Think about the different accents and tones of voice being used – what do these tell you about Tom and Lynda?

6 Does listening to the studio recording add anything else to your understanding of the scene? Think particularly about the following:
- Are Tom and Lynda's voice levels loud or soft?
- Do their voice levels change? If they do, at which points in the script and for what reasons?
- Are pauses or other breaks in conversation used in any important way?
- How do you know *where* the scene is taking place? Are any sound effects used? How are they used?

Moving on

Although neither are present, both Phil and David Archer are mentioned in the scene you have just read. From what is said about them there, and from reading the storyline notes and programme outline for Scene Four, predict how this next scene might go.

Write out the possible dialogue between Lynda, Phil and David, linking up what has happened and pointing forward to new story possibilities.

The Story of An Hour

Kate Chopin was born Katherine O'Flaherty, in St. Louis, Missouri, in 1850. Her father died in a train crash when Kate was very young and she was brought up in an all-female household – mother, grandmother and great grandmother.

In 1870 she married Oscar Chopin, who worked in the cotton business. They lived in New Orleans and then in rural Louisiana.

Kate was unconventional in her choice of clothes and in her enjoyment of long, unaccompanied walks around the streets of New Orleans; yet she enjoyed a happy marriage, had a wide circle of friends, and was seen as a loving wife and devoted mother of six children.

Oscar Chopin died in 1882. Kate started to write in the same year.

The Story of An Hour was written on April 19th, 1894. It was not published in Kate Chopin's lifetime. She died of a brain haemorrhage in 1904.

Before Reading

What does the title and the first paragraph of this story suggest it may be about?

"Knowing that Mrs Mallard was afflicted with heart trouble, great care was taken to break to her as gently as possible the news of her husband's death."

Talk this through in pairs and then write down what you think will happen in the story, as a series of short notes.

The Story of An Hour

Knowing that Mrs Mallard was afflicted with heart trouble, great care was taken to break to her as gently as possible the news of her husband's death.

It was her sister Josephine who told her, in broken sentences, veiled hints that revealed in half concealing. Her husband's friend Richards was there, too, near her. It was he who had been in the newspaper office when intelligence of the railroad disaster was received, with Brently Mallard's name leading the list of "killed". He had only taken time to assure himself of its truth by a second telegram, and had hastened to forestall any less careful, less tender friend in bearing the sad message.

She did not hear the story as many women have heard the same, with a paralysed inability to accept its significance. She wept at once, with sudden, wild abandonment, in her sister's arms. When the storm of grief had spent itself she went away to her room alone. She would have no one follow her.

There stood, facing the open window, a comfortable, roomy armchair. Into this she sank, pressed down by a physical exhaustion that haunted her body and seemed to reach into her soul.

She could see in the open square before her house the tops of trees that were all aquiver with the new spring life. The delicious breath of rain was in the air. In the street below a peddler was crying his wares. The note of a distant song which some one was singing reached her faintly, and the countless sparrows were twittering in the eaves.

There were patches of blue sky showing here and there through the clouds that had met and piled one above the other in the west facing her window.

She sat with her head thrown back upon the cushion of the chair, quite motionless, except when a sob came up into her throat and shook her, as a child who has cried itself to sleep continues to sob in its dreams.

She was young, with a fair, calm face, whose lines bespoke repression and even a certain strength. But now there was a dull stare in her eyes, whose gaze was fixed away off yonder on one of those patches of blue sky. It was not a glance of reflection, but rather indicated a suspension of intelligent thought.

There was something coming to her and she was waiting for it, fearfully. What was it? She did not know; it was too subtle and elusive to name. But she felt it, creeping out of the sky, reaching toward her through the sounds, the scents, the colour that filled the air.

Now her bosom rose and fell tumultuously. She was beginning to recognise this thing that was approaching to possess her, and she was striving to beat it back with her will – as powerless as her two white slender hands would have been.

When she abandoned herself a little whispered word escaped her slightly parted lips. She said it over and over under her breath: "free, free, free!" The vacant stare and the look of terror that had followed it went from her eyes. They stayed keen and bright. Her pulses beat fast, and the coursing blood warmed and relaxed every inch of her body.

She did not stop to ask if it were or were not a monstrous joy that held her. A clear and exalted perception enabled her to dismiss the suggestion as trivial.

She knew that she would weep again when she saw the kind tender hands folded in death; the face that had never looked save with love upon her, fixed and grey and dead. But she saw beyond that bitter moment a long procession of years to come that would belong to her absolutely. And she opened and spread her arms out to them in welcome.

There would be no one to live for her during those coming years; she would live for herself. There would be no powerful will bending hers in that blind persistence with which men and women believe they have a right to impose a private will upon a fellow-creature. A kind intention or a cruel intention made the act seem no less a crime as she looked upon it in that brief moment of illumination.

And yet she had loved him – sometimes. Often she had not. What did it matter! What could love, the unsolved mystery, count for in the face of this possession of self-assertion which she suddenly recognised as the strongest impulse of her being!

"Free! Body and soul, free!" she kept whispering.

Josephine was kneeling before the closed door with her lips to the keyhole, imploring for admission. "Louise, open the door. I beg; open the door – you will make yourself ill. What are you doing, Louise? For heaven's sake open the door."

"Go away. I am not making myself ill." No; she was drinking in a very elixir of life through that open window.

Her fancy was running riot along those days ahead of her. Spring days, and summer days, and all sorts of days that would be her own. She breathed a quick prayer that life might be long. It was only yesterday she had thought with a shudder that life might be long.

She arose at length and opened the door to her sister's importunities. There was a feverish triumph in her eyes, and she carried herself unwittingly like a goddess of Victory. She clasped her sister's waist, and together they descended the stairs. Richards stood waiting for them at the bottom.

Someone was opening the front door with a latchkey. It was Brently Mallard who entered, a little travel-stained, composedly carrying his grip-sack and umbrella. He had been far from the scene of the accident, and did not even know there had been one. He stood amazed at Josephine's piercing cry; at Richards' quick motion to screen him from the view of his wife.

But Richards was too late.

When the doctors came they said she had died of heart disease – of joy that kills.

After Reading - First Impressions

Now that you have read the story, stay in pairs and discuss the following statements.

This story is mainly about:

● a woman's mixed reactions to the death of her husband (A)

● a broken marriage, which would have failed anyway (B)

● the difficulties some people have in showing their true feelings (C)

● the problems in being "a loving, devoted wife and mother" (D)

● the dangers of shocking someone with a weak heart (E)

● a selfish woman who gets what she deserves. (F)

If you wish, add a statement of your own which suits the story better than any of those provided.

After you have discussed each statement, rank the statements in order, based on how far you agree with them.

Start with the statement you agree with most and end with the statement you agree with least.

Quickly write down your reasons for placing these statements in your particular order. Remember to use evidence from the story to support your views.

Reading Closely

Now that you have read and considered the story in some detail try the following tasks:

1 Louise Mallard's changing feelings are complicated. Write down what you think her thoughts were at three important points in the story:

a) when she heard the news of her husband's "death"

b) when she was sitting alone by the window in her room

c) when she saw her husband walk in through the front door.

Note: "moment b" takes up a lot more of the story than either "a" or "c".

2 The story ends: "When the doctors came they said she had died of heart disease - of joy that kills."

What do you think is meant by this sentence?

Why do you think the doctor came to this conclusion?

Does the reader, in this case, know more than the doctor?

What effect does the ending have on the story as a whole?

Language Focus

This story was written in 1894. Inevitably, many of the words and phrases are no longer used in everyday speech. For example, towards the end of the second paragraph you will find the phrase "hastened to forestall" where a modern version might use "hurried to prevent".

There are many other examples to consider, from single words like "yonder" or "fancy", to whole phrases such as "her bosom rose and fell tumultuously". List as many as you can find and suggest modern alternatives. The list has been started for you:

DATED	MODERN EQUIVALENT
intelligence	news
hastened to forestall	hurried to prevent
yonder	
fancy	
her bosom rose and fell tumultuously	

Writing for Television

1 Return to those three important moments identified in "Reading Closely".

Take each of the scenes in turn and present them in storyboard form, shot by shot, as visual sequences for a television or video version.

2 You are now in a position to rewrite the whole story as a television script.
Work from the visual ideas explored in your storyboards.
Work steadily from scene to scene, considering:

● the setting - where the action is taking place

● the characters - how they look and behave

● the action and dialogue - what and how things are said.

How would your television version differ from the written original?
What would you want to keep?
What would you want to change?

STORYBOARD AND FILM AND TELEVISION SCRIPTS

For practical help with storyboards and writing a television script, use the sheets *Making a Storyboard* and *Film and television scripts* in the **Heinemann English Assessment and Reference File.**

Now read the television script by Kathleen Potter.

The Story of An Hour by Kate Chopin

Modern day dramatisation for television by Kathleen Potter.

SCENE 1. INTERIOR. LOUISE'S BEDROOM 5:00 PM

THIS IS THE BEST BEDROOM IN A MODERN HOUSE, A MIDDLE INCOME BARRATT TYPE. THE WHOLE PLACE IS IMMACULATE AND IT IS DECORATED IN A VERY FEMININE STYLE; MATCHING CURTAINS AND BEDCOVER, A LARGE DISPLAY OF SCENT BOTTLES AND MAKE-UP ON THE DRESSING TABLE. THERE ARE RUCHED AUSTRIAN BLINDS AT THE WINDOW, WHICH ARE AT PRESENT HALFWAY DOWN SO THE ROOM IS DIM. IN A CORNER NEAR THE WINDOW IS AN UPHOLSTERED BEDROOM CHAIR. WE SEE ALL THIS AND COME TO THE BED. ON THE BEDSIDE TABLE ARE, CONSPICUOUSLY, SEVERAL BOTTLES OF PILLS, A BOOK ABOUT HEART ATTACKS, A CLOCK THAT SAYS 5 PM, A LARGE WEDDING PHOTO OF BRENTLY AND LOUISE AND A GLOSSY Woman MAGAZINE. ON TOP OF THE BED LIES LOUISE, DRESSED BUT WITH HER EYES CLOSED AND SO STILL SHE MIGHT ALMOST BE DEAD.

OVER THIS WE HAVE THE TITLES CAPTION.

THE DOOR OPENS GENTLY AND JO POKES HER HEAD ROUND, CHECKING TO SEE IF LOUISE IS AWAKE. JO IS LOUISE'S SISTER, A COUPLE OF YEARS OLDER, HAS JEANS AND A BUTCHER'S APRON ON: SHE HAS OBVIOUSLY BEEN COOKING.

LOUISE OPENS HER EYES AND TURNS HER HEAD AS JO COMES IN. SHE IS CARRYING A CUP OF TEA.

LOUISE:

Is that the time? Bren'll be home soon.

JO:

Don't worry. You know he's never early.

LOUISE:

Never late either.

OF THE TEA, GRATEFUL.

You shouldn't have.

SHE SITS UP, JO WILL PUT THE CUP DOWN AND PULL UP THE PILLOWS SO LOUISE
CAN SIT UP AGAINST THEM, AS PEOPLE DO IN HOSPITAL.

JO:

I thought I'd give you plenty of time to get ready.

LOUISE:

OF THE APRON.

I was going to get up and do the supper.

JO:

You'll be better for having a rest. I've left you the salad to do.

LOUISE:

Right (WILL DO)

JO:

Let's make you comfortable. Then you can drink your tea. And you've got nearly an
hour before his train gets in. It's all right. You must try to relax.

LOUISE:

You sound like the doctor.

HARSHLY, FROM DOWNSTAIRS THE TELEPHONE HAS STARTED TO RING. JO, STILL
PLUMPING THE PILLOWS, REACTS.

MIX TO

SCENE 2. INTERIOR. HALL 5.20 PM

JO OPENING THE DOOR TO RICHARD. HE IS BREN'S FRIEND, FORTYISH, LOOKING DISTRESSED. JO TOO IS DISTRESSED, OBVIOUSLY SOMETHING HAS HAPPENED.

RICHARD:

I came as quick as I could. I didn't want anybody else to get here first.

JO:

It's good of you to come.

RICHARD:

Have you told her?

JO:

Not yet, I thought two of us.... (WOULD BE BETTER)

You are sure?

RICHARD:

I've checked, it was his train, they put one of those phone numbers on the screen.

JO:

It could kill her.

RICHARD GRIPS HER ARM TO SILENCE HER: LOUISE IS COMING DOWNSTAIRS. SHE HAS CHANGED HER FROCK, DONE HER HAIR, LOOKS LOVELY. JO AND RICHARD LOOK AT HER, STRICKEN. LOUISE SEES THEIR FACES, IS ALARMED.

LOUISE:

What's the matter?

JO:

NERVY.

Nothing....

LOUISE:

You look as if you have seen a ghost.

RICHARD:

You musn't upset yourself.

WHICH DOES, OF COURSE, UPSET HER.

LOUISE:

Why not? ALARMED. What's he doing here? TO JO OF RICHARD, REALISING IT'S ODD. There's something going on isn't there?

JO:

You're going to be very brave.

LOUISE:

ALARMED. Is it Bren?

JO:

We're not sure what's happened....

SEE RICHARD'S FACE. HE'S CHECKED.

LOUISE:

Has there been an accident?

JO:

We think there might have been. There was a news flash....

RICHARD:

To say his train's crashed.

LOUISE:

REALISING. Oh no!

JO:

We haven't found out the details.

LOUISE:

WITH CERTAINTY AND IN DESPAIR.

He's dead.

RICHARD:

I have checked.

LOUISE'S FACE CRUMPLES, SHE COVERS IT WITH HER HANDS, ROCKS BACKWARDS AND FORWARDS WITH THE PAIN.

LOUISE:

Bren, Bren...not my Bren...not him....

JO IN TEARS GOES TO HER, TRIES TO HOLD HER.

LOUISE:

I can't do without him. TURNS INTO JO'S ARMS SO THEY CLING TOGETHER, WEEP TOGETHER. RICHARD, IN THE BACKGROUND, IS EXCLUDED.

FROM RICHARD

MIX TO:

SCENE 3. INTERIOR. BEDROOM 5:40 PM

LOUISE COMES IN ON HER OWN, CALMER NOW. SHE CLOSES THE DOOR, LEANS BACK AGAINST IT, WEARY, TEAR STAINED, DISHEVELLED. WE HOLD HER GRIEF FOR A MOMENT, SEE HER BREATHING BEGIN TO CALM. SHE FROWNS A LITTLE AS IF PUZZLED AT HER FEELINGS, WILL TURN AND LOCK THE DOOR.

CUT TO:

SCENE 4. INTERIOR. BEDROOM.

TIME HAS PASSED. LOUISE IS IN ANOTHER PART OF THE BEDROOM. HER MOOD HAS CHANGED AGAIN. GRIEF. (DESPAIR?)

SCENE 5. INTERIOR. BEDROOM.

TIME HAS PASSED, LOUISE IS BY THE BED WITH THE PHOTO OF HER AND BREN. SHE PUTS THE PHOTO DOWN, FROWNS AGAIN AS IF PUZZLED AT HER FEELINGS. LOOKS AT THE WINDOW. SHE WALKS TOWARDS IT STEADILY, PULLS THE BLIND FULLY UP.

SPRING SUN COMES IN, THE ROOM IS SUDDENLY MUCH LIGHTER. SHE LOOKS OUT, DRAWS A DEEP BREATH, BLINKS AS IF SEEING IT ALL AFRESH. WE HEAR THE TWITTERING OF BIRDS AND A WOMAN SINGING.

THE SUN IS ON HER FACE.

LOUISE:

TO HERSELF.

It's all out there (VOICE OVER?)

THE WORLD OUTSIDE THE WINDOW SEEMS OPEN AND WELCOMING. WE SEE HER APPRECIATE IT. SUDDENLY ELATED.

Waiting. For me. (VOICE OVER?)

THE DOOR HANDLE RATTLES. LOUISE, DISTURBED, TURNS.

JO:

(OUT OF VISION)

Louise.

LOUISE DOESN'T ANSWER. LOOKS BACK THROUGH THE WINDOW, NOT WANTING TO BE DISTURBED.

JO:

(OUT OF VISION)

What are you doing?

THE DOOR HANDLE RATTLES, LOUISE LOOKS AT IT, THEN BACK, BUT NOW LESS CALMLY, TO THE WINDOW.

JO:

(OUT OF VISION)

You'll make yourself ill.

LOUISE LOOKS AGAIN AT THE RATTLING HANDLE, NOT WANTING THIS.

JO:

(OUT OF VISION) ANXIOUS.

For heaven's sake, let me in.

AND NOW SHE BANGS THE DOOR. LOUISE STARES AT IT.

JO:

(OUT OF VISION)

You know you must be careful.

LOUISE HOLDS HER HANDS OUT AS IF TO WARD OFF THIS ENCROACHMENT.

LOUISE:

Go away. Leave me alone. You're as bad as Bren....

THE BANGING STOPS, THERE'S A SUDDEN SILENCE AS WE SEE LOUISE REALISE THE IMPLICATIONS OF WHAT SHE'S SAID.

CUT TO:

SCENE 6. OUTSIDE THE BEDROOM/INTERIOR BEDROOM. CONTINUOUS.

JO IS THERE, SILENCED BY WHAT LOUISE HAS SAID. SUDDENLY THE DOOR OPENS. LOUISE WILL REACH FOR JO.

LOUISE:

UPSET. I didn't mean it.

JO:

It's all right.

LOUISE:

It isn't that I didn't love him.

JO:

I know.

THEY GO TOGETHER INTO THE ROOM.

LOUISE:

I did most of the time. SHE WILL LOOK TOWARDS THE WINDOW; WE SEE THE SUN, THE OPEN SKY.

LOUISE:

He needed me to come home to. He needed me to be here.

SHE LOOKS AROUND THE ROOM. SUDDENLY, IN CONTRAST TO THE SKY, IT LOOKS FUSSY AND CLUTTERED.

JO:

And you always were.

LOUISE:

Yes. SHE LOOKS AT JO, DARE SHE SHARE WHAT SHE'S REALLY THINKING? BUT JO KNOWS.

LOUISE:

A DEEP BREATH. Now I don't have to be. I can go where I want, be how I want. ELATED. It's my life.

MIX TO:

SCENE 7. INTERIOR. HALL 5:55 PM.

RICHARD IS ON THE PHONE TO THE DOCTOR. STILL, OF COURSE, DISTRESSED.

RICHARD:

... all right Doctor, I'll do my best... thanks a lot, as soon as possible.

HE PUTS THE PHONE DOWN. THE DOOR IS ALREADY OPENING. HE LOOKS
AMAZED, AT BRENTLY ENTERING WITH A BAG.

BRENTLY LOOKS EQUALLY AMAZED. BREN RECOVERS FIRST.

BRENTLY:

What're you doing here? ANXIOUS. Nothing the matter with Louise is there?

RICHARD:

No, but...

BRENTLY:

Thank God. I missed the train. I had to get a taxi.

BEHIND RICHARD IS A SOUND, HE TURNS, SEES LOUISE AND JO COMING
DOWNSTAIRS, LINKED TOGETHER. RICHARD STEPS IN FRONT OF BRENTLY.

RICHARD:

TO BREN.

Be careful.

IT'S TOO LATE. WE SEE LOUISE'S SHOCKED FACE. SHE SWAYS.

JO:

To Bren. How did you... (GET HERE?)

BRENTLY:

ALARMED. Louise.

HE PUSHES PAST RICHARD. LOUISE HAS NOW SAGGED AGAINST JO, JO IS TRYING TO HOLD HER.

BRENTLY:

She's fainted.

RICHARD:

I told you to be careful.

LOUISE IS NOW ON THE FLOOR, BREN KNEELING BY HER, FRANTICALLY TRYING TO REVIVE HER.

BRENTLY:

Louise, Louise, it's only me....

She hasn't fainted (SHE'S DEAD).

RICHARD:

It was seeing you. The relief. Her heart just couldn't take it.

SEE JO'S FACE: SHE KNOWS IT'S NOT THAT SIMPLE.

Your Version

How does your television version compare with Kathleen Potter's? Consider those three important moments in each version. How do they differ? Which do you prefer and why?

Through Other Eyes

The Husband's Story by David Stafford presents the same basic story but seen through the eyes of the husband, Brently Mallard. Before reading this alternative viewpoint and from what you have already learnt about Brently, predict what his version of the events might be. Remember to focus on his thoughts and feelings towards his wife, Louise, as well as his actions during the course of his day.

The Husband's Story

Shot 1. MLS BRENTLY sitting
Shot 2. Ms BRENTLY
      TIGHTEN to MCU

Note

MLS = Medium long shot

MS = Medium shot

MCU = Medium close-up

The Husband's Story
by David Stafford

BRENTLY SITTING ON CHAIR

BRENTLY: Driving along the motorway with my sweet wife Louise at the weekend, doing no more than sixty-five, when a squirrel runs out in front of me. Well, what was I supposed to do? Swerve into the crash barrier and write the Volvo off? For a squirrel? Slam the anchors on and be responsible for a multiple pile up?

My sweet wife Louise clearly thought I should have done. She was of the opinion that squirrels are wild, free creatures with a right to life. I pointed out that the coachload of Everton supporters behind us were also wild free creatures whose equal right to life would have been severely endangered had I trod hard on the brake pedal at that particular inopportune moment. Louise grew sullen and, even though I had my eyes on the road, I know she was giving me That Look.

So this morning I phoned the Department of The Environment. I spoke to a chap called Noris who suggested I'd be better off phoning the Health Ministry. He said they'd probably know. So I phoned the Ministry of Health and ended up speaking to a Mrs Inman who said as far as she knew they were. So there you are. It's official. Grey squirrels are vermin. They are not an endangered species. They are not protected by any Act of Parliament.

I was feeling pretty triumphant when I put the phone down and then I realised that Derek Wheeler - he sits at the next desk - he'd been listening to every word. He wanted to know the full story. So I had to tell him.

Do you know, Derek Wheeler laughed at me. He laughed out loud. He thought it was very funny, the trouble I was going to to score a tiny point in a row with my wife. He said I was being petty minded.

He doesn't know Louise. Louise never rows or argues. There's never a raised voice or even a proper exchange of ideas. Sometimes she doesn't even have to speak: just a tightening of the lip.. a quickening of the breath... a clouding of the bright eye that says, "You Are Making Me Suffer." She could make a saint feel guilty. A doctor once told her that she had a slight heart complaint and I'm made to feel guilty about that every day.

I won't crow or be pompous. I'll just mention it as an interesting piece of information I've come across during the day. Over dinner, perhaps.

"Oh by the way, grey squirrels are vermin. I checked. They damage trees. You save a lot of trees by killing a squirrel."

It won't do any good, of course. I know I'll just get a blank stare as if she doesn't know what I'm talking about. Then later on, when she's sure I'm looking, she'll ostentatiously stroke/secretly take a couple of her heart pills and stare out of the window as if she's looking for death to come down the drive in a Vauxhall Astra and take her off to squirrel heaven.

When we first got married I...I admired... she had a spirit.. a naughty gleam in that bright eye. A wildness. Perhaps I did too. You grow up don't you?

And now I've missed the train and I'll be late home. She'll give me hell for that. Oh, she won't shout at me or threaten me or hit me: no, not my sweet wife Louise. No. Anger and bluster are not the weapons in her armoury. She has infinitely more subtle, more devious weapons. She'll think of some sort of hell to give me when I get home, though. Some way to make my life a misery.

After Reading

"The Husband's Story"

Does it differ from your own predictions?

Does it fit with your interpretation of the original story?

How does Brently treat his wife?

How might she feel about the way he treats her?

What kind of a life do they have together?

Which moments from which version did you prefer?

Support your views by referring to both texts.

What If?

From your understanding of the characters, what would have happened if:

a) Brently had died in the accident?

b) Louise and Brently had both lived?

c) Brently had been told that Louise had died in an accident.

After discussion, choose one of the above alternatives and write that variation of the story.

IT'S A CRIME

Most people are on the right side of the law most of the time. All the same, no one is perfect: even the most careful driver goes over the speed limit sometimes or parks illegally. What should happen when someone breaks the law? And how can crime be discouraged? This unit looks at these issues and more.

Them and us

Read the article on the opposite page.

Were you surprised at the results of the Melbourne investigation or does it confirm what you thought?

1 Pick out the details from the survey that are different from your own experience.

2 Pick out the details that seem to be similar to what you have seen in your own community.

3 What, in your view, are the major student crime problems:
   • in school
   • outside school?

4 The article reports on one area which appointed police constables to schools. How well did this work?

5 Would the same system work in the schools you know? Why or why not?

6 What would you do about student crime in the schools and communities you know?

Responding to crime

Most people agree that crime should be discouraged. The problem is finding the best way of doing this. Offenders usually end up with a fine and/or a stretch in prison. Some young people's first visit to court ends simply in a warning. Others may find themselves put on probation or placed in an Intermediate Treatment scheme which is a demanding programme of projects and counselling designed to change criminal habits.

The extracts on the following pages each look at a different way of dealing with crime, past and present. Read them carefully and note down the different punishments or treatment. If you are given information about the nature of the crime, write that down as well.

906 students questioned, one found innocent

Anne Susskind

A survey of Melbourne schools has revealed that almost 45 per cent of students have stolen from their fellows and done so, on average, seven times. This, and other startling statistics, were reported at a conference on adolescent crime organised by the Australian Institute of Criminology.

Mr Shane Carroll, who conducted the survey of 906 girls and boys at Melbourne's state and independent high schools, told delegates that results also showed 60 per cent of students had damaged school property an average of 22 times.

About a third had stolen either from their family or their school and all but one of the students questioned had committed at least one offence.

Mr Carroll said the adolescent self-report studies revealed more illegal behaviour than indicated by official police and court statistics.

He said adolescents avoided police attention because many adults did not report their crimes.

"People do not report young offenders for many reasons, including a belief that they can deal with the youth themselves," he said.

The New South Wales education department's head of community relations told the conference that arson and vandalism on trains and schools in the state cost the taxpayer more than $16 million (about £7 million) a year.

He said that sophisticated protection methods did not seem to be an effective deterrent. Fifty schools recently installed expensive electronic surveillance systems which were subsequently attacked by 77 people.

In the Northern Territory, 13 schools have employed full-time uniformed police constables. The principal of one of these schools, Mr Roy Harvey, said his constable had become indispensable.

Vandalism had almost disappeared, trespassing was no longer a problem, and students felt safer, he said. They approached the police on issues ranging from broken hearts and loneliness, to fights, rape and malnutrition.

Mr Harvey said: "Kids don't talk to their parents any more. Often parents work, or they are not on the same wavelength as adolescents. But the child wants to talk to an adult.

"They could talk to a teacher, but they want adults from the real world," he continued.

In contrast to official statistics, the survey suggested that social class and gender were not significant factors.

Professor Maurice Balson, from Monash University, said teachers should stop blaming poverty, unemployment and parental problems for adolescent crime.

Instead, they should try to involve students in school activities, consulting them in the planning of disciplinary procedures, for example. Only when students felt they had a worthwhile place in society would they cease this violent behaviour.

from The Times Educational Supplement

A glimpse into history

The ways in which crime has been dealt with have changed over the centuries. Two centuries ago, nearly every country viewed public execution as an important way of discouraging crime. Another way to warn people of the dangers of crime was by a public whipping.

In 1862, one of the cases that came before the courts in Cardiff involved an 11-year-old boy who had been caught stealing a basket worth two pence in Bridge Street. The story behind the theft was this.

The child had come to Cardiff from Ireland with his elder brother who had found work as a seaman. The elder brother had placed the youngster in lodgings and had given the landlady money in order to look after him until his return from sea. Months passed and the brother failed to return. The money ran out and eventually the boy was thrown out of his lodgings onto the street. Soon he became desperate with hunger and stole the basket in order to buy bread.

When he was in court the judge asked the 11-year-old if he would like to be found work on a ship as a cabin boy. He said that he would rather be sent home to his mother. Although there was much sympathy for the boy in the courtroom, he was sentenced to a public whipping.

COURTS WILL STING THE RICH

COURT fines which sting the rich but go easy on the poor are to be announced shortly by the Government.

Magistrates will multiply the amount of spare cash an offender has each week by a number of points, calculated according to the seriousness of the offence.

So a shoplifter on social security with £5 left at the end of the week might be fined 15 weeks' disposable income - a total of £75.

A better-off shoplifter, with £15 a week to spare, would also be fined 15 weeks' disposable cash - a total of £225.

The new scheme has been tried out at Bradford, Basingstoke, Swansea and Teesside for up to fourteen months.

Chris Coupland, deputy justices' clerk at Bradford Court, said: "It means the poor are paying sums they can actually manage."

Daily Mirror
Tuesday 16 January, 1990

Michael Robinson:

Crime reparation schemes

The double benefit when criminals meet victims

Criminals and their victims are being brought face to face in a series of pilot schemes backed by the Home Office. The aim of the schemes is to help both the offender and the offended.

It was bitterly cold last month when James Pearcey was taken to jail. He'd been involved in a serious arson. There'd been a grudge over an unpaid debt and the fire was started as a way of getting even. Because of the fire, he was on his way to the Thorpe Arch remand centre, near Boston Spa in Yorkshire. Not because he was the arsonist. In fact, James Pearcey was the arsonist's victim. It was his flat that had been set alight while he was asleep in bed. The man who did it, Peter Barry, was due to go to court the following week and was on remand in custody in Thorpe Arch, waiting for his one-time friend to arrive.

They had agreed to meet as part of a new Home Office-backed experiment where the parties to a crime, victim and offender, are brought face to face in an attempt to make good some of the damage done between them. The Home Office has been encouraged by evidence from America which suggests that successful face-to-face meetings do benefit both sides. Victims have the chance to come to terms with what has happened to them and even to ask for direct compensation. Offenders are made to face up to the person they harmed. They get the chance to apologise and make amends.

On top of that, it is hoped, the protective barriers of excuses which they erect to justify their actions will be broken down. Burglars, for example, often argue that victims were themselves to blame because they'd left the window open, or that no real harm had been done because the insurance would pay, or that a victim was financially better off and so could afford the loss. Last summer in Leeds, the Baker family were burgled four times in just five weeks. The insurance paid out, but Sue Baker became convinced she was being watched - on one occasion, the burglar had broken in while she was out of the house for just 20 minutes. Seven-year-old Samantha wouldn't sleep in her room for a week after a burglar got in through her window; six months later she's still suffering nightmares. Simon, who was nine at the time of the burglaries, still refuses to go upstairs on his own. According to his father, that's a complete change in his character.

Alan Baker decided to take part in the Leeds scheme - one of four the Home Office is funding to meet one of the men who had burgled his house. He's a solicitor and is used to dealing with criminals. But this was the first time he'd met one who had harmed him directly.

It was the first time for the 24 year-old burglar, as well. He'd never met one of his victims, and, minutes before the meeting, he was nervous almost to the point of hysteria about the prospect. 'What's he going to say? What's he going to do?' he kept asking. He stood up and sat down again, one moment smiling with bravado, the next looking as if he was on the point of tears. He had the right to leave, since neither side is forced to take part. But in the end he decided to go through with the meeting.

It lasted about 40 minutes. Alan Baker confronted the burglar with the effect on his family, and thinks that his message sank home. The burglar apologised for what he'd done and passed on some useful tips about making the Bakers' house more secure. Then he went on to explain his own problems. He wanted to go straight but there was no work for him in Leeds. He had the chance of a roofing job in London which would give him less temptation to burgle again. But he couldn't take it since his probation order restricted his movements.

Would Alan Baker support his request for his probation order to be relaxed? Despite being one of the man's victims, Alan Baker said he would. He thought the man meant what he said. From the legal point of view, he's well aware that what he thinks doesn't matter. Nonetheless, he thinks his opinion should be taken into account.

from The Listener 20 February 1986

Punishment to fit the crime?

1 Which punishment do you think is most likely to deter the criminal from committing a similar crime again? Why?

2 Which is most likely to deter other people from committing the crime? Why?

3 Which approach takes the circumstances of the offender into account?

4 Which approach aims to help the victims as well?

5 What sort of punishments would you impose for the following offences:
   • vandalising a children's playground
   • taking an old lady's purse from her shopping bag
   • glue sniffing?
   Explain the thinking behind your judgments.

6 What do you think makes a fair punishment for a crime?

Assignments

Most material on crime is written by the police or by people who work closely with them. Some police have felt for years that they do not hear enough about what young people think. You have been given the opportunity to put that right in your locality by providing material to help train new police officers. Choose one of the following:

• **A short leaflet or talk about vandalism**
   Try to explain why people do it and how their energies could be channelled in a different way.

• **Shoplifting: the inside story**
   A short article or cassette that investigates why some young people are attracted to shoplifting, how they first get involved and how some of them have been able to stop.

• **"It's not always us that are wrong, sometimes the law itself is wrong."**
   An article for a police magazine. Focus on two or three aspects of the law that do not seem entirely fair to you. For example, some people feel that changes could be made to the law that allows the police to move people on when they are just standing around.

• **Making our place better**
   A talk or article about making where you live a better, safer, crime-free place. Include what the government, the police, adults and young people can do to make this happen. Use illustrations if possible.

• **An open letter to a new police officer**
   expressing young people's feelings, hopes and fears about the police.

At the end of your work, write a brief introduction which explains to your reader/listener why you completed the assignment in the way you did. For example, if you produced a cassette, explain why you thought that was a good way to communicate your message.

A DAY
IN THE LIFE

Like his father and grandfather, Robert Maltby farms 289 acres in Dorset. No two days are the same but this is Anna Pavord's report of one summer day on the Maltby farm. It was originally written for *The Observer* newspaper's colour supplement.

6.15^{am} Listen to "Farming Today" on Radio 4. Look at the weather and juggle with the jobs to be done. Get into van and drive to the farmyard, a short distance from the house.

7.00^{am} Start feeding the pigs, which are housed in pens (some under cover) around the farmyard. This is a daily routine, Christmas Day and all. The 48 sows get ground barley and protein, while the 150 young pigs get Ultragrow pellets. In the covered farrowing house 12 sows with young litters are kept warm under the infrared bulbs. Muck out all the pigs and pile the dung behind the piggery ready to load into the muck spreader. The dung will later be used as fertiliser in the fields. Talk to Kenny, the farm worker, about his jobs for the day. He will top off the rank growth of nettle and thistle from the pastures with the Massey Ferguson tractor and cutter.

9.00^{am} Back for some breakfast – muesli, bacon and eggs, toast, coffee – and phone calls. Think about pigs; check the price per pound with two wholesaling meat companies. The price for pork fluctuates daily. In hot weather it is difficult to sell in the shops, so the price may drop.

10.00^{am} Back to the farmyard. Notice that sheep are bunching in a corner of the field. Why? Must check later. Unhitch a trailer loaded with gates and hurdles from the second tractor and drive the tractor round to the piggery to hitch up the dung spreader.

10.20^{am} Sort out a bird scarer from equipment stored in an old railway carriage in the yard. It's the Flash Harry kind with one fluorescent orange vane that turns in the wind. Walk to a 32 acre field of winter barley and dig the scarer support into the flinty ground. Set the scarer on top and spin it into the wind. Rooks have been doing some damage – eating the ripening grain of the barley. This may keep them off. Pick a few ears to test: the grain is still liquid, but should be set ready for cutting in about three weeks' time. The barley will then be ground up for pig food. It is an excellent crop, but there is still the threat of a flattening summer storm. At harvesting the grain will be separated from the straw and there should be a good few loads of straw to use for cattle bedding in winter.

11.00^{am} Work on the sileage pit in the farmyard. Sileage is cattle food made by cutting green grass and packing it into a pit. Robert finishes covering the pit with black polythene, weighted down with hundreds of old tyres. He watches the rooks flying over his barley, sizing up the bird scarer.

11.30 **am** Wheel the weighing machine into a pig shed to weigh five pigs that should be ready for slaughter. "Nice long pigs," says Robert. He catches each one by an ear and heaves it in to the weighing machine. They are all round about the 140lb mark, but the amount of useable meat on them works out at about 100 lb an animal. After weighing, each pig is marked with a blue aerosol spray.

11.40 **am** Straw up a newly boarded and creosoted pig house and move pigs from an adjoining house into this clean one. Move a feeder into the new quarters and fill up with Ultragrow pellets. Robert talks to the pigs all the time: "Get your noses out of there, pigs. What's up with you then."

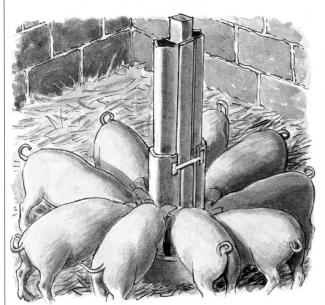

11.50 **am** Into the van to look at the cattle a couple of fields away. Robert immediately notices one cow standing apart from the rest. "I'll bet she's calved", he says, and drives over to that corner of the field. On the verge by the fence is a black and white calf. Robert jumps out of his van with a tin of equipment and catches the little bull calf. With an instrument he fixes an elastic band very tightly round its testicles. This stops the blood supply, so that the testicles will eventually wither and drop off. Then he tags the calf's ear with his herd number and its own number. The rest of the herd have gathered closely around and Robert inspects them briefly. He is pleased with the calf, a Hereford cross, which will go well in the market.

12.00 **pm** Off to look at the sheep who have been a bit neglected recently because of the haymaking. Thirty-five lambs went off to North Devon Meat Company last week. Robert thinks about

the numbers to go off next week. He tours the field slowly in his van, and checks on a white bundle that turns out to be some loose fleece but might have been a dead lamb. Seven lambs have squeezed under the gate into the adjoining field. Robert drives them back to join the flock. 198 ewes with their lambs. He aims at an average of at least one and a half lambs per ewe. They are mostly Suffolk cross Scotch half breeds crossed with a Dorset Down ram.

12.20 **pm** Put on leggings and boots and visit rams, penned up together in a neighbouring paddock until their annual bout with the ewes comes around in October. After a struggle, Robert catches one, right hand clutching the loose skin behind the back leg, left arm under the ram's chin. He upends it onto its feet with a knife. He has been thinking about dipping them, but the weather is too uncertain. The dip may be washed out by rain.

12.50 **pm** Down in the van to an outlying 39 acres of land where some young Charolais cross steers are grazing. Robert shifts the electric fence down the length of the field to give the cattle a fresh strip of grass. He will cut the rest of the field, five or six acres, for hay. He has already got 2,446 bales under cover from the 27 acres he has cut. In an exhausting three-day haul he got it all carted in before the weather broke.

1.10 **pm** Back for lunch. Beef curry, rice, popadums, salad, gooseberries and caramel custard. Listen to the weather forecast, do some paper work, think about pig prices.

2.00 **pm** Two men turn up from the North Devon Meat Company, to talk in the farmhouse about meat supplies and bonuses. They stay for an hour. Afterwards Robert telephones to order five tons of pig feed. He also arranges for the pigs he weighed earlier to be collected by the Dorchester Meat Company. The price is down on his last sale, but it is unlikely to get any better.

3.20 pm Back to the farmyard where two sales representatives from a seed merchant are waiting. They talk about barley seed and try to interest Robert in the possibility of flying in turnip seeds over his barley. The plane flies low, dropping 6lb turnip seed and 4lb slug pellets an acre. The seed germinates before the corn is cut and has a month's headstart over seed sown after harvest. Robert is dubious.

3.40 pm Fits a new infra-red bulb in the farrowing house. One sow is overdue. Robert tries her teats to see if any milk is being produced and checks the date that she was with the boar.

3.45 pm The truck arrives to load the pigs. Jerry the driver has some hair-raising stories, mostly involving bulls. "Those will kill out well," he says approvingly as the pigs come grunting up the tailboard, which is disguised with straw. They will be in the butchers' shops within three days.

4.00 pm Starts to creosote another pigpen. "I've been trying to tart up the pig department recently." Robert says. He mucks out the pen from which he had moved the pigs earlier in the day.

4.45 pm Time to feed all the pigs again. He checks the 12 sows and their litters in the farrowing house. He thinks about weaning five litters of pigs the following day so that he can get the sows back to the boar. Each sow needs to have two litters a year for the pigs to be profitable.

5.15 pm Separate the new calf and its mother from the rest of the herd and walk them over several fields to join another group of cattle. The Charolais bull is with this group and Robert wants the cow to get in calf again as soon as possible. He has great respect for this bull. A vast creamy monolith of an animal. It turns its head a fraction to note the arrival of mother and calf but otherwise takes no interest. Walk back over the fields between neolithic barrows and tumuli and move the first herd of cattle through into new pasture. Soon the rain will bring fresh grass to the fields recently cut for hay. Catch up with Kenny on his tractor and talk about the day: it is only the second time the two have met that day.

6.00 pm Shut the gates of the farmyard and return to the house for tea with his wife and one of his two young sons. Wholemeal bread and jam, sponge cake, fruit cake, lots of cups of tea. Think about the next day. Perhaps there will be time to clean out the sheep dip.

7.15 pm Over to a neighbour's land three miles over the hill where Robert has got some cattle. He had recently put his Hereford bull in with them and wanted to check that all was well. On to a local pub with his neighbour for a couple of pints.

8.45 pm Back for supper - grapefruit, plaice, strawberries, cheese and biscuits. Afterwards watch the news and listen to the weather forecast.

10.45 pm Bed. Think about the weather, pig prices, dipping the sheep and a family holiday, first one for 13 years. Rapidly go to sleep.

Reactions

1 What, if anything, surprised you about life on the farm?

2 What appealed to you about the Maltby's way of life? Why?

3 What jobs would you have most wanted to avoid if you were the Maltby's eldest daughter or son? Why?

4 What qualities do you think you need in order to be this type of farmer?

5 Why do you think the newspaper chose this piece for the young people's section of their magazine? Does it succeed in appealing to your age group?

Selections

The **Observer** printed a very full account of one day in Robert Maltby's life. Many magazine editors would feel that this report was too long for their readers. On your own, think about how you might edit it to make it suitable for a magazine for 14 - 16 year olds.

1 Are there any entries that could be removed altogether? Make a note of which ones they are and why you think you could do without them.

2 Are there any entries which could be reduced to two or three words instead of taking a whole paragraph?

3 Are there any entries that you think it is important to keep untouched? Why do you think these need to be printed in full?

4 In your view, are there any gaps in the information that the reporter collected for her article? If so, what are they?

Discussion

1 Using your answers to the questions in *Selections*, discuss in your group how this article might be edited. Try to agree on these points:
  • entries that could be removed entirely
  • entries that could be drastically cut *(choose between four and six of these)*
  • entries that are worth highlighting *(choose between three and five of these)*
  • good photographs to accompany the article *(choose about four).*

2 Discuss how this material could be adapted for use in an information book, designed for seven year olds. Try producing the first chapter of such a book.

Writing

Write your own *A Day in the life* for a magazine of your choice. You do not have to name it but say what sort of magazine you are aiming at. For example, you might choose to write for a careers magazine for school leavers. You could base your article on your own experiences or interview someone about their job, for example:
  • a parent or relative
  • an older friend
  • a housewife or househusband
  • a neighbour or a friend of the family
  • a youth club leader or teacher.

HELP

For guidelines on interviewing see *Sita and Mary* and **Heinemann English Assessment and Reference File**, pages 91 and 92.

DRAFTING
To get the most out of your work:
First draft: keep it readable.
Review: listen to the comments of others and check it yourself.
Final draft: produce a revised best-possible version.

Alternatives

1 Write down what you imagine is a typical day in the life of the person you want to interview and then compare it with the real thing. (For example, your idea of what a "typical" housewife/house-husband does might be very different from what actually happens.)

2 Interview two people in the same profession or doing a similar job and see how their accounts compare.

WASTE LINES

I learnt a lot from that article.

I suppose so, but I nearly fell asleep reading it!

To get your information across in a way which ensures that people read it and understand it, you have to find ways of presenting it which suit:
- what you have to communicate – your information or message
- why you want to communicate it – your purpose
- who you want to communicate it to – your audience.

This unit explores techniques of effective communication using three pieces of writing on the same theme – waste and recycling – but written for very different audiences.

Mountains of Waste

How many things will you throw away today? The box from a new tube of toothpaste? The empty cereal box or milk carton? Your bus ticket? Perhaps a crisp packet and an empty drink can? Start a list of the things you throw away in one day and you'll be amazed at how long it becomes.

Each year the average British family throws out:

- waste paper which took around six trees to make

- more than 500 cans, of which 300 are food or pet food cans

- 47 kilos of plastics, 32 kilos of metals, 45 kilos of food and 74 kilos of glass.

That means that each of us is throwing away more than ten times our body weight in rubbish every year.

Packaging

Almost one-third of our rubbish comes from packaging of different sorts—paper, glass, metal and plastic. Packaging is important—it protects products and ensures hygiene—but a lot of packaging is simply there to catch our eye, to make us buy this rather than that. What we should be careful about is how much we use and how much we throw away.

One way to cut down on waste is to recycle wherever possible. That means putting bottles in bottle banks and finding somewhere to take old newspapers. Another way is to re-use. That means, for example, returning milk bottles to be cleaned and used again or, where possible, returning soft-drink bottles to the shop from which they came.

Glass

Glass is largely made from sand—and there's hardly a shortage of that in the world. However, the sand has to be dug up and this leaves unpleasant gashes in the landscape. More importantly, glass-making uses enormous amounts of energy. Much less energy—and much less sand—is used if old glass is recycled—melted down to be made into new bottles and jars.

Every tonne of crushed waste glass used saves the equivalent of 135 litres (30 gallons) of oil. So by taking used glass to your local bottle bank you really are helping the environment. Don't forget—you can take more than just bottles; empty jam jars will do as well, but remember to take the lids off first!

Paper

Britain uses the wood from more than *130 million* trees a year to make paper and cardboard for such things as newspapers, magazines, junk mail, kitchen towels, tissues and boxes. It takes a lot less time to use these things and chuck them out than it does to grow another 130 million trees, even if they are fast-growing softwoods such as pine. Britain only grows about 10 per cent of the trees it uses.

The manufacture of paper uses tremendous amounts of energy and can cause much pollution from poisonous wastes which kill wildlife when they find their way into rivers and seas (see page 24). And when land is cleared for plantations of trees, wildlife habitats are lost.

115

Metals

Some tin cans are made partly of tin, but they also contain steel and, increasingly, aluminium. All these metals have to be mined from the ground and this can be damaging to the local landscape. Since the 1950s, manufacturers have made the tins thinner, using less material, and this has helped. But we could be doing much more, particularly by recycling the metals we use.

Aluminium is made from a mineral called bauxite. It takes four tonnes of bauxite to make *one* tonne of aluminium. Aluminium is used for making drinks cans and for such things as milk bottle tops, some takeaway and frozen food containers, and the little cups used, for instance, to hold some individual fruit pies. Also, of course, the foil which many cooks wrap around the turkey at Christmas.

Aluminium can be melted down and recycled again and again. This saves enormous amounts of energy and bauxite. We should try not to use too much aluminium, but, when we do, recycling it is one of the ways we can best help the environment. And you can make some money doing it! (See page 78.)

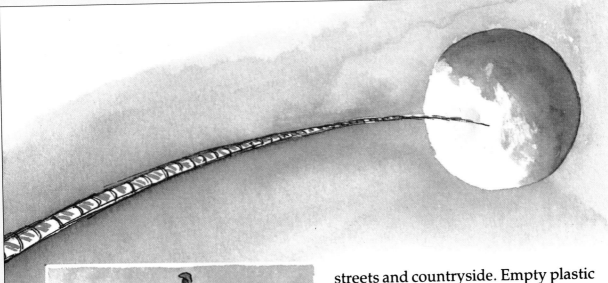

streets and countryside. Empty plastic bags and bottles can even be found in Antarctica and on the slopes of Mount Everest.

One of the problems with plastics is that they are not fully biodegradable. That means they don't rot and disappear completely. So food that we consume within minutes is wrapped in materials which last for hundreds of years!

You can now get plastic bags designed to break up slowly when they are thrown away but they do not yet disappear entirely.

Believe it or not
Every single day, Britain produces enough rubbish to fill Trafalgar Square—up to the top of Nelson's Column.

Plastics
Well over a third of the packaging we use is made from plastics. There are over 50 types, made from non-renewable materials such as oil, coal and natural gas. In Britain very little of this plastic is recycled. It goes into our dustbins and ends up in holes in the ground. The rest lies around in our

YGC Action

Watch out for over-packaging, e.g. small packets of crisps inside larger packets. Re-use plastic carrier bags. Better still, use a cloth bag. Recycle by collecting glass and paper products and aluminium cans and taking them to your nearest collection point.

31

What the passage says

1 List the eight or nine reasons which the article gives in favour of recycling materials.

2 Why do you think the article is organised into five major sections by the use of sub-headings?

3 In pairs, discuss and make notes on which section made the strongest impression on you and why.

4 Re-read the four "Believe it or not" boxes. Why are these distributed throughout the article in this way?

5 When you first read the article, did the boxes interrupt your reading or did they help you follow the argument? Again, discuss and make notes.

How it says it

1 Look closely at the way language is used in this article. Are there any words or phrases you do not understand?

2 Do you think the language is aimed at a particular audience, and if so, which audience? What makes you think this?

3 Think about the design and layout of the article. Do you find it attractive and helpful, or confusing and off-putting? (It might help to compare it with the article which follows, **A Clean Sweep.** What differences strike you immediately?)

4 **A Clean Sweep** is aimed at the readers of an adult newspaper – from a design point of view, what audience do you think **Mountains of Waste** is aimed at?

5 You have now considered the audience for the language and the audience for the design of this article. Do they match? Do they have to – or can good design widen the audience for a piece of writing?

A Clean Sweep

This is an edited version of a much longer article from the Nottingham Evening Post. It is a detailed, sometimes technical, piece of writing, explaining some of the local consequences of complicated new legislation on litter and waste. It is about 900 words long.

A clean sweep

April 1st saw the introduction of tough new laws aimed at beating the litter problem which blights our town and cities.

The Environmental Protection Act brought in sweeping changes to the way councils and other bodies must now act to combat litter.

The legislation marks a significant shift in the way councils tackle the problem of litter and breaks new ground in the approach to its clearance.

For the first time it sets out uniform standards of cleanliness which have to be achieved in different locations - like town centres and residential areas - and under different circumstances.

Councils, schools, colleges, Government departments and British Rail now have clear duties.

It is a unique Act - no other country in the world has such national legislation governing litter.

Litter isn't just an eyesore - it is also dangerous. Dog faeces can lead to blindness: broken glass and cans pose a potential threat: a discarded crisp packet can cause a cow to choke to death.

Yet millions of tons of rubbish are still dropped in Britain every year - at a cost of millions of pounds to the public.

Five thousand tons of litter alone are dropped on Britain's motorways every year - the equivalent of six full dustcarts every working day.

Litter takes years to break down - a cigarette takes one to five years, a ring pull from a can takes 80 to 100 years and a plastic bag 10 to 30 years.

Education

The failure of numerous education projects to persuade people not to drop litter in the first place prompted the tough legislation.

"We have tried the carrot now we need a bit of stick," says a Department of Environment spokesman.

"Litter is filthy, nasty stuff which is bad for business and bad for our health" adds Andrew Blackall from the Tidy Britain Group.

"We are in danger of becoming the dirty man of Europe. There is no stigma connected with dropping litter in Britain - yet it is very anti-social, gross and obscene.

"We are all responsible and we can all do something about it".

New duties

The law places new duties on councils, schools and transport authorities who all now have a duty to keep areas clean to a set standard.

And it also gives local authorities a new duty to clean roads.

To enable them to carry out their duties, the Government has produced a code of practice which works on the basis of four new grades of cleanliness and different zones of land.

There are 11 different zones covering town centres, high and low density residential areas, all other areas, educational institutions, beaches, railways, roads, towpaths, waterways and shopping centres, plus four standards of cleanliness.

Grade A is litter free. Grade B is mostly clear, apart from small items. Grade C is widely littered. Grade D is heavy litter.

The law lays down set time limits in which councils have to clear rubbish once a complaint is made, depending on the grade of litter and type of area involved.

"You would not expect the same frequency of litter in a suburban area as you would in a city centre shopping area so the different zones and time limits take account of that," explained a DoE spokesman.

As a yardstick the dirtier an area the quicker it has to be cleaned.

Maximum

Councils themselves can now serve litter abatement notices against individuals or organisations who don't meet deadlines for clearing rubbish.

They can also designate private land to which the public has access as litter control areas. This means the owner has to take responsibility for clearing litter or face prosecution.

Councils also have the power to introduce litter warden schemes. Wardens can issue on-the-spot fixed penalty fines of £10 if they see someone dropping litter.

This is based on a pilot scheme run in the City of Westminster which proved highly successful.

And anyone convicted of flouting litter laws faces a big increase in the fine they have to pay. Under the new law the maximum fine for convicted offenders has been raised from £400 to £1000.

From May 1, local authorities will have to clear up dog faeces from land.

And from June 1, shopkeepers and businesses can be served with street litter control notices by councils if their shop fronts are littered due to the nature of their business, for example fast-food restaurants.

The notice can lay down how many bins should be provided and other cleaning tasks which have to be carried out.

The legislation also clamps down on abandoned shopping trolleys. Local authorities now have the power to round them up and charge owners for their return.

The idea is to persuade supermarkets to bring in deposit schemes for the trolleys to stop them being abandoned in the first place.

GET A GRIP ON LITTER

THE NATIONAL SPRING CLEAN 19-28 APRIL

continued on next page

A **Clean Sweep** continued from previous page

Category zone		CLEANLINESS STANDARD			
		A	B	C	D
1	Town centres		6hrs	3hrs	1hr
2	High density residential		12hrs	6hrs	3hrs
3	Low density residential			12hrs	6hrs
4	All other areas			1wk	60hrs
5	Amenity beaches		MAY SEPTEMBER		
6	Motorways and main roads			4wks	1wk
7	District and local roads			2wks	5days
8	Education institutes			24hrs	
9	Railway embankments within 100m of platform ends			2wks	5days
10	Railway embankments within urban areas other than in 9			6mths	3mths
11	Canal towpaths in urban areas			2wks	5days

Maximum time limits for restoring to an acceptable grade of cleanliness

● *Countdown to cleanliness. How the time limits work for each grade of litter density*

In the editor's chair

1 Working individually or in pairs, continue to edit the article, down to a new maximum of 300 words. Your audience is now a teenage magazine rather than a local evening newspaper! You need to decide what information needs to stay and what can be rejected according to what your audience will find interesting or relevant. The article will need to be organised and presented differently.
Can you improve on the title - **A Clean Sweep?** What about sub-headings, pictures or diagrams? Can you think of other ways of making the layout interesting and attractive?

2 Your reworked article will appear on page six of next week's edition. The editor has allowed you 25 words, on the front page, to attract attention to your inside article. Write an eye-catching and informative 25 word paragraph, complete with a short headline, to introduce your piece.

NEWS REPORTS
Advice and support on writing news reports is available in **Heinemann English Assessment and Reference File**, pages 80 and 81.

Popular science?

This is an extract from a GCSE Science investigation, which looked at some of the environmental advantages glass bottles have over plastic ones.

RECYCLING: PLASTIC VERSUS GLASS

"Plastic waste causes a lot of problems and recycling is obviously a good idea. In some towns there are bottle banks where you can put used glass bottles. But as yet there are no plastic banks; this is partly because glass is easier to recycle than plastic.

All clear glass is made from the same chemical compounds and after being sorted by colour, it can be broken into small pieces and added to the ingredients used for making new glass, thereby saving energy and raw materials.

Plastic waste, however, can be a mixture of many chemical compounds. Some plastics only contain carbon and hydrogen (polythene, polypropene and polystyrene), but others contain chlorine, oxygen and nitrogen (pvc and nylon). The first type of plastic can be broken down chemically and used again. But at the moment, it is very expensive to separate the compounds in the second type.

Since it is sometimes difficult to distinguish between the two types, plastic tends not to be recycled in the same way as glass. Perhaps some new thinking is needed here?"

Nasreen Akhtar (15)

Transform the information in this extract into a short, entertaining magazine article aimed at a general readership.

Supply a suitable title which reflects your approach: *Bank on Glass – Plastic hasn't got the bottle*, perhaps, or *A load of old rubbish?* Try to achieve a light hearted, non-technical tone, perhaps by using a *Did you know?/Believe it or not* style of presentation.

Pulling it all together

Using everything you have learnt in this unit, write a full length feature article or scientific report on the problems of waste and recycling.

1 Decide on the purpose of the piece – for example, a General Science GCSE Assignment or an article for a serious magazine.

2 Decide which information to use. You will not be able to include everything presented here, and you may wish to include extra information you have researched yourself.

A local angle could give a useful focus for the piece.

Whichever approach you choose, the task is to identify:

* *what* you want to say,
* *who* you want to say it to, and therefore
* *how* you are going to say it.

GREATER
APPLICATION NEEDED

Kevin Daughtry is not having much success in finding a job. After two hundred and eighty-five failures, he decides to change his tactics. Unfortunately his imagination soon gets the better of him...

```
                                                          391 Boltham Road
                                                          Boltham
                                                          Lancashire
     Personnel Manager                                    2nd January 1992
     Pinedale Ltd
     Pine Mill
     Franklin Heath
     Manchester


     Dear Sir
     I am writing in response to your advertisement in the MANCHESTER EVENING POST for a trainee Quality
     Control Assistant. It caught my eye the other day as I was flicking nonchalantly through the paper in
     search of the financial section. It struck me at the time, that I would probably be the ideal person
     for this job.

     You state in the advert that the applicant should be 18 or over, with O Level Maths and English and
     at least one A Level. Well, I'm your man. I am definitely 18 or over, I have ten O Levels (including
     Maths and English), and no less than five A Levels.  Quite apart from my academic achievements, I am
     honest, hard working, enthusiastic and loyal. My previous experience is vast, and should come in very
     handy in the field of quality control. In other words I know quality when I see it!

     On leaving school I attended Oxford University for three years, where I studied Philosophy,
     Sociology, Greek Mythology and Quality Control. When I left Oxford I moved around quite a bit, trying
     to find the type of employment that suited me best. To date, I have worked in printing, engineering,
     design, catering, management and the civil service, as well as being a librarian for several months.
     I also spent six weeks in Egypt examining the Pyramids. This was followed by two years in the British
     Army stationed overseas, where I enjoyed a multitude of outdoor pursuits, including wind surfing,
     bareback riding, cycling, powerboat racing, shooting and mountaineering.  Whilst in the Himalayas, I
     was involved with an expedition to climb K2, the highest mountain in the range and was particularly
     interested in the quality of the sleeping bags, because if they hadn't been well made we would all
     have frozen to death, and I would not be writing to you now.

     So if you still have any doubts as to whether I am suitable for this job, let me quell them by saying
     that I'm prepared to work for exactly half as much as you are offering.  I will enjoy the good
     working conditions, and as far as 'good prospects for advancement' are concerned, I think you only
     have to look at my list of achievements so far, to realise that I have indeed got good prospects.

     I would be very surprised indeed if you did not invite me in for an interview because, as the
     Americans would say, "You'd be passing up a real tomato"!

     I look forward to hearing from you.

     Yours sincerely

     Kevin Daughtry
     Kevin Daughtry
```

If you were the employer, what would you think?

On this occasion, Kevin gets the sort of answer that fits his letter almost perfectly!

Pinedale Ltd Pine Mill
Franklin Heath Manchester

Kevin Daughtry
391 Boltham Rd
Boltham
Lancashire

Dear Kevin

Thank you very much indeed for your wonderful letter; I may have it framed. Unfortunately, I have to tell you that you have not been included on the shortlist for interview. The fact is, we had forty five thousand million applicants for the job, so I'm afraid that narrowed your chances somewhat.

Although you are obviously a talented and well travelled young man, there were certain qualifications which we required, that due to lack of space, we were unable to include in the newspaper advertisement.

First of all, the successful applicant had to have swum the English Channel at least twice, with the complete twelve volume set of the Encyclopaedia Britannica tied to his ankles. Also, as well as free fall parachuting (at which you are obviously an old hand) he must have dived off the top of the Empire State Building into a thimble full of washing up liquid, whilst simultaneously constructing a scale model of the Eiffel Tower in matchsticks during his descent.

There were also one or two other minor points which let you down. We really needed someone who could speak thirty two different languages fluently, had been to Oxford and Cambridge and got honours degrees in at least fifteen subjects, and most importantly, we wanted someone with six arms, who could do the jobs of three men and thus save the company money.

Thank you for your interest however, and may I suggest that you try Hollywood, where I believe they are already planning the making of the next 'Superman' movie.

Yours sincerely (and good luck!)

Steve Radcliffe

Steve Radcliffe

So what do employers actually want?

In order to answer that question, we spoke to several managers about what they looked for in job applicants. The interviews are on the cassette and some of their advice is included on this page.

I look for orderly thinking.

I look for accuracy...I am very particular about neatness.

Sales Manager

Administration Manager

I want something that makes it look as if the person has thought, 'Who am I applying to?' and, 'What is the job?'

Keep it simple, keep it short, keep it correct...plus a little personal touch.

Customer Services Manager

Promotions Manager

Don't go into tremendous detail: that can be done at an interview.

Does that person have some qualities that I am looking for in this job?

The first impression is important.

Administration Manager

Customer Services Manager

Sales Manager

MAKING AN APPLICATION

There are two main ways of presenting yourself
in an initial written application for a job:

THE CV AND COVERING LETTER

A CV (or Curriculum Vitae if you use its full Latin name) is a brief outline of what you have done so far in life. Ideally, most employers like it on a single side of A4 paper. A common format is shown below:

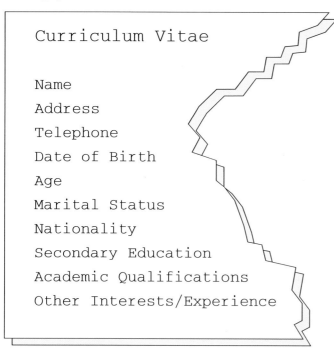

```
Curriculum Vitae


Name
Address
Telephone
Date of Birth
Age
Marital Status
Nationality
Secondary Education
Academic Qualifications
Other Interests/Experience
```

If you include a CV, the covering letter adds a short personal touch. One manager we spoke to was quite happy to receive a single paragraph letter with a CV. This letter might simply say how interested you are in the job and when you would be available for interview/to start.

THE LETTER OF APPLICATION

This is still the way in which many employers will expect you to apply for a job. One manager said: "I need a letter that is reasonably short and that is basically three paragraphs." Those paragraphs can be summed up like this:

One: Introduction

Employers need to know for which job you are applying. Many will also like to know where you saw the advertisement or heard about them.

Two: About Yourself

You need to say who you are, what you can do and what experience/ qualifications you possess.

Three: Conclusion

Apart from making clear your interest in the job, an employer needs to know when you are available and where you can be contacted.

WARNING!

Read the job advertisement carefully to see whether or not a CV is required. If it is not made clear, the choice is up to you. In all other cases, follow the instructions. Some employers like the simplicity of the CV whilst others prefer the traditional application letter.

HELP

A completed CV and a photocopiable blank CV form is available in **Heinemann English Teacher's Pack 4**.

Can you do better than Kevin?

Look at the job advertisements and choose one to apply for.

Before drafting your letter, make notes about what you could include in it, such as the subjects you are currently studying, any relevant work experience and any special interests or achievements. Ask a friend to check this in case you have left out anything important.

When your notes are ready, write your letter. The layout in Kevin's letter and in the reply may help you.

DRAFTING

To get the most out of your work:

First draft: keep it readable.

Review: listen to the comments of others and check it yourself.

Final draft: produce a revised best-possible version.

Doing it Kevin's way

Once you have written a letter that might actually get you a job, it can be fun to have a go at doing it Kevin's way.

In pairs, each take any advertisement you wish (or make one up that appeals to you) and write the most unlikely and exaggerated letter that you can invent. Swap application letters and try your hand at a reply.

More Kevin

If you want to read more of Kevin Daughtry's letters and find out what eventually happens to him, you will need to find *In Reply to Your Advertisement* by John Kirkbride (Andre Deutsch: ISBN 0 233 98344 9 or Puffin Plus: ISBN 0 14 034128 5).

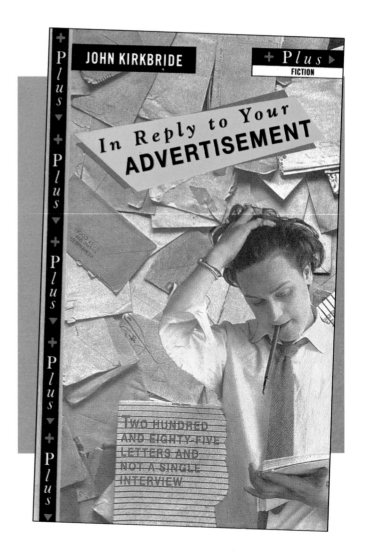

Job advertisements

SCHOOL LEAVER WANTED
To care for two young children. Must be genuinely interested in working with children. Contact Mrs Simpson, 29 Caffield Street, Wilmston WW5 6PD.

HALLS *LEATHER GOODS*
Require
FULL-TIME JUNIOR SALESPERSON
Will need to be able to work flexible hours and must be of smart appearance.
Apply to Halls Leather Goods, St Julians Shopping Centre, Wilmston.

MAYBEE RECORDS
Packers needed
New staff required for packing of videos, tapes, CDs and T-shirts.
Strength not important but speed and accuracy are.
Initial inquiries to Mr D Jayex, Personnel Department, Maybee Records, PO Box 35, Wilmston WW4 8HB.

MAKE BRITAIN BEAUTIFUL
International Nutrition and Health Company require 3 self motivated young people to help introduce a revolutionary new computerised diet programme.
Further details from XS Products, PO Box 74, Wilmston WW1 9DD.

PRYDERI COMPUTERS
Require an office assistant to undertake general duties.
Experience of office work would be an advantage but is not essential.
Familiarity with specialist computer language would be a bonus.
Pryderi Computers, Staffing, City Road, Wilmston WW2 7UG.

COLLEGE HOSPITAL - UPPER WILMSTON
THEATRE ASSISTANT
As a supporting service for the operating theatre, the postholder will be required to wash, re-pack and sterilise used instruments. Some work will be undertaken in the theatre itself.
Applicants are not expected to be experienced in this type of work.
Full training will be given.
Please contact The Personnel Department, College Hospital, Ilton Road, Upper Wilmston.

JUNIOR SECRETARY
International company require bright youngster for general office work.
Will include some typing and wordprocessing.
Opportunities to travel for the right candidate.
Contact Sally at Intro Personnel, Chapel Street, Wilmston.

ME AND MY LANGUAGE

The following passages were written by two students on how their use of language changed as they grew up.

Watching my language

I was born in Sneinton near Nottingham, and at the age of eighteen months, moved the short distance to live in Bakersfield. I have never lived anywhere else.

Obviously, where I have grown up has affected the way I use the English language. It has also given me the accent I have. Since so much of early life is spent at school, this has also had a big effect on the way I speak.

I don't believe that I speak too badly but I am aware that when I am with my friends, I speak very differently compared to when I am with parents or teachers.

It is interesting to discover that accents can vary over very short distances. For example, my Grandparents have lived in Hucknall all their lives, and although Hucknall is only eight miles from Nottingham, they use very different words and phrases to us. When I go and visit them, they don't say "Hello love", they always say "Ey up me duck". I have also found that in Mansfield, about twelve miles away, the accent is different again.

My dad is Spanish, and around the home he speaks Spanish because my mum can understand it. My dad's English is not too good, he finds it hard to pronounce certain words. When some of my friends come round to my house, they find it difficult to understand my dad and they wonder how I can. I guess it is just because I am used to it, I don't speak much Spanish but I can understand my dad alright. I suppose it must have influenced the way I speak but I'm not sure how.

I have a cousin who lives in Newcastle and I think his accent is brilliant. The last time I went up there I was just getting off the train and a middle aged man said to me: "Have y' got t' time laddy?", in a really strong Geordie accent. "Yes, three o'clock", I replied. "U' a canny lad", he said. "Canny", I said to myself, what on earth does that mean? When I got to my cousin's house, that was the first question I asked him. Much to my amazement he told me that it meant kind or nice! Like most people, I don't consider myself or others from my area to have much of an accent. But it would be very interesting to know how we sound to someone from Birmingham, Newcastle or Liverpool.

By Daniel Balaguero 15

Me and my language

Throughout my early years language was one of the most important skills to aquire. As an Asian, I lived within an Asian society at home and with relatives, but outside the family I had a different life style, encountering different religions and other races. The language spoken outside the home was English, whereas within the family I spoke Punjabi and a little Urdu.

As a toddler, I first began to speak in Punjabi, as I was influenced by the people around me, mainly my mum, dad, brothers and sister. I began to talk when I was approximately eleven months old. My first words were not those I was repeatedly taught by my family but sounds – "ha, ha", "da, da" and "mm, mm".

By the age of two, I could respond reasonably well to my immediate family but only in Punjabi and a little Urdu. I only began to pick up English words and phrases when I started at nursery school. At this time I still could not respond in full sentences. For example, I would not have said "Can I have that?", "This is mine" or "I want yours". But rather, "That", "Mine" and "Want".

By the time I was four, I could respond more fully but again,mainly in Punjabi.

Keeping in touch with two or possibly three languages was not hard for me at the age of five. I was not in any danger of forgetting them, because at home I spoke Punjabi and Urdu and at school, English.

However, my parents were worried that at this age the more you learn about a language and a culture the longer it stays with you. And my brothers, my sister and I frequently spent up to six hours in school, five days a week, saw a wide range of English programmes on television and played with a lot of English friends. My parents were not against this but they were worried that English would take over and that we would leave our own language and culture behind. As a result they constantly provided us with books in Urdu, to improve our own language and to learn more of our culture.

A little later I also started Arabic lessons. I attended an Arabic class five days a week, each day after school. Every Muslim child must learn to read Arabic in order to read the Qur'an – the Islamic holy book. It took me five years to learn Arabic.

By now I had learnt four languages, Punjabi, Urdu, English and Arabic. But my language learning was not to stop there.

When I reached secondary school I was confronted with another language – French. I was not too keen on this subject at first but the good side was that it wasn't only me or a minority of pupils learning this language, we all were. This made it so much easier for me. It made me more confident because we were all in the same boat, I could practise my French with other pupils around and it helped both them and me.

Languages have clearly played a very important part in my life.

By Nazea Asmat 15

My changing language

Now plan a similar account of your own.

1 Begin by making a list of the important influences which have affected your language, from when you were a young child up to now.

2 Discuss these questions with a partner, and add to your list any other ideas which come out of this discussion.

3 Ask your parents and grandparents about the earliest developments in your language, and add to your notes any information they can give you.

4 Using your notes, take it in turns to present your own language history to your group. Listen carefully to other people's stories and comment helpfully on them. Some of their ideas may help your own language biography.

5 Combine these comments and examples with your notes, to prepare a final written account of "Me and my language".

The following questions will help you get started:

• Where were you born? Does this affect the way you speak?

• Have you ever moved from one area to another? Did the move change the way you spoke?

• Has your education influenced the ways you use language?

• Do you use a local dialect? Always? Sometimes? Never?

• Have you ever been teased about your dialect or accent?

• Do you vary your language depending on whom you are talking to?

• Do you have any other languages which affect when, where and how you speak English?

HELP
The accompanying cassette contains the students talking about language change. The sheets on accent and dialect in **Heinemann English Assessment and Reference File** on pages 53 to 54 will also be useful.

AUTISM
- A WORLD APART

Channel Four recently made a television documentary with **Autism a World Apart** as its title. The following comments are taken from that programme:

Presenter

"When Debbie was fourteen months old, this normal toddler's behaviour underwent a complete change. She stopped all eye contact with her mother, with all adults, with all children. She cut herself off from the world around her. No-one knew what had gone wrong.

Doctors were consulted. Different theories were tried, were rejected. Two years later Debbie was finally diagnosed as being autistic. Debbie, lives literally, in a world apart."

"I'd say to her as a baby, 'Debbie' I'd say, and she would look at me and smile. And then suddenly she wouldn't look at me. I said, 'Debbie, Debbie, look at me' and she would turn around and she would fight me from trying to get a look at her. And that is so alien in a little baby. They at least want to look at you even if they don't want to do what you are asking."

Mother

Presenter

"In 1944 the American psychiatrist Leo Kanner first used the term 'early infantile autism' to describe symptoms he had observed in some of his patients. Even now, Kanner's characteristics of autism remain essentially unchanged.

Generally, it starts before a child reaches thirty months. There is always abnormal social interaction and language development. And the child exhibits a considerable need for stereotyped behaviour and repetitive routine."

"It's almost impossible for the normal person to conceive of the strange world inhabited by the autistic child. A child who may have little or no sense of themselves as a person. A child who certainly has no social sense, or interest, or even understanding of other people as people."

Psychiatrist

Mother

"The strain in living with a child who is autistic is phenomenal. And I think, probably greater than most other handicaps, because autistic children look so normal. And yet the very fact that they are not interested at all in social relationships, that they are perfectly content to be alone, is very, very wearing."

"Some experts say that brain damage is the cause of the disordered behaviour of the autistic. That in some way the chemicals that make the brain work aren't functioning properly, causing a blockage in the normal transmission of information through the brain.

Others, noting that four out of five autistic people are male, and also that the male foetus develops later than the female and is thus more prone to brain damage, again suggest that this is the root cause of this difficult condition."

Presenter

"There is no conclusive evidence that all autistic children are brain damaged. And in fact, there is evidence to the contrary. Many of the children who come to us have had exhaustive tests and no brain damage is revealed."

Psychiatrist

"Another way of looking at autistic children's behaviour is to say that they are extremely fearful children, extremely insecure children and they react to that insecurity by avoiding contact. And they become prematurely independent. They become far too independent, far too young.

We know that the causation of autism is probably different in different children and that it takes all sorts of factors to produce autism. But what is happening with these children is that very often when they are upset, when they are distressed, they do not go to their parents for comfort, they go away."

Psychiatrist

"If she doesn't improve by the time she's twenty or so, it's going to be a real problem for her. She's not going to be able to mix very well in the community. She certainly won't be any good with boyfriends. Goodness knows what we are going to do."

Mother

These nine statements reflect very different viewpoints on the problems faced by autistic children and their parents.

Autism – seen through whose eyes?

Read through the statements again, then answer the following questions:

1 What are the main points/arguments put forward by each of the contributors? Make brief notes outlining them.

2 Are there any important differences between them? How would you describe these differences?

Looking at language

The language used by each contributor is also very different. For example, the mother uses language directly and dramatically: "I said, 'Debbie, Debbie, look at me' and she would turn around and she would fight me from trying to get a look at her." The psychiatrist uses less personal language: "Many of the children who come to us have had exhaustive tests and no brain damage is revealed."

1 Working in pairs, discuss and then write down some of the different ways language is used by these speakers.

2 Why do you think these differences occur?

3 Which statements do you find the most powerful or the most interesting? Why do you think this is so?

Autism – the facts

These are some of the materials produced by the National Autistic Society, an organisation seeking to increase awareness and understanding of autism and so strengthen the lobby for improved facilities for autistic people.

WHAT IS AUTISM?

Autism is a perplexing life-long mental disability which often occurs with other disorders, including mental retardation. It affects four times as many boys as girls. Autistic conditions vary from profound severity to subtle problems of understanding.

About four to five people in 10,000 will have classic autism, 15 to 20 per 10,000 will have autistic-like conditions.

Autism impairs the whole process of communication. Those affected cannot recognise or interpret everyday messages and signals: facial expressions, gestures and different tones of voice. Without these basic tools of communication,

they are isolated in a world of people and concepts which are confusing. Many develop secondary problems which include:

- indifference to other people
- difficulties in acquiring any form of communication
- problems in learning
- problems in adapting to the demands of everyday life
- a narrow, repetitive, stereotyped pattern of behaviour.

In marked contrast to these are the "islets of ability". Many people with autism, who may be severely disabled in most areas, will display an extraordinary talent for, say, music or art, mathematics or mechanics.

Children with autism go through various phases. Behaviour is often difficult and the autistic pattern is in its most typical form when children are two to five-years-old.

Some improvement in sociability, skills and behaviours, can be expected from six to 12. Problems may reappear or become more marked during the teens and twenties but difficulties tend to lessen again in later life.

Out of every 100 children with autism, five to 10 will become independent as adults, 25 to 30 will make good progress but still need support and supervision. The rest may remain severely disabled.

The National Autistic Society

THESE PIN MEN HAVE BEEN SELECTED TO ILLUSTRATE SOME OF THE DIFFERENT WAYS IN WHICH AUTISM IS DISPLAYED.

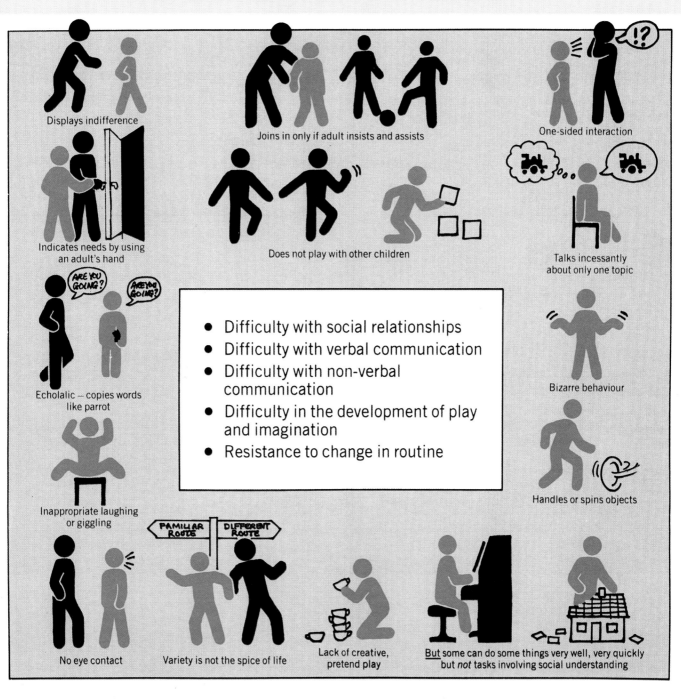

Becoming clearer

1 Did you learn anything more from these materials? If so, add them to your existing notes.

2 Now rearrange your notes under headings such as *Symptoms*, *Behaviour*, *Extent*, *Possible causes*, *Effects on other people*, etc.
This will help you to pull out exactly the information you want when tackling the following activities.

3 Use your notes to do one of the following tasks:
   a) Prepare a talk to a group of students your own age on the subject of autism, explaining what autism is and how it affects individuals and their families. Use audio and visual aids if you consider them to be appropriate.
   b) Design and produce an attractive, illustrated leaflet which explains some of the facts about autism to an audience of 14 to 16-year-olds.
   c) Plan a short video charity appeal for the National Autistic Society, aimed at an upper school audience (14 to 16 years).

Produce an outline description for the appeal as a whole, and a television script and storyboard breakdown for at least two of its scenes.

> **HELP**
> For practical help on television scripts and storyboarding see the **Heinemann English Assessment and Reference File**, pages 95 to 99.

Dustin Hoffman playing the role of autistic adult Raymond Babbitt in the film **Rain Man**. Tom Cruise plays his younger brother Charlie.

SORTING IT OUT

Making notes is a skill that develops best with practice. Brains do not work identically and people make the notes they need in the way which suits them best. You need to decide how to organize your own notes so that you can make them quickly but still understand them when you go back to them later. You also need to select the most useful information to note down. This unit looks at selecting and organizing information for notes.

The following passage is part of a history lesson about how the first atomic bomb came to be produced and used. It is followed by the notes written by three students setting out what they saw as the key facts.

> **NOTE**
> There are exercises using the cassette which it would be useful to tackle BEFORE going on to the rest of the unit. **See Heinemann English Teacher's Pack 4**.

The First Nuclear Bomb

In 1939 three scientists fled to the United States of America with knowledge that would change the course of history. Albert Einstein, Leo Szeland and Enrico Fermi left Europe to escape persecution and brought with them information about the potential for a new atomic or nuclear bomb.

Almost immediately after their arrival, President Roosevelt was warned of the dangers if Hitler were to succeed in creating such a bomb but did very little about it. It was only after America had entered the war herself in 1941 that Roosevelt set up a research establishment to develop the idea. The work went well and expanded quickly so that a new location was needed which was provided at Oak Ridge in Tennessee. Final tests were arranged at Los Alamos in New Mexico, using the site of an old school. The first explosion took

place on the 16th of July 1945 and was seen 250 miles away. The initial flash of that explosion turned into a purple and orange fireball. When scientists returned to the site after the explosion they found that the tall tower which had been built to hold the nuclear device had vaporised.

The successful test gave President Truman a way in which he believed that the war with Japan might be ended swiftly with America in a strong position at any peace negotiations. On 6 August 1945 a B29 plane was despatched to Hiroshima under the command of Colonel Paul Tibbetts, carrying a nuclear bomb. It was 8.15 in the morning when the plane reached Hiroshima, took aim and opened the doors that released the 10,000 lb device. Forty three seconds later, it struck.

Looking at the notes

1 Which set of notes do you think is easiest to follow?

2 Which set of notes is hardest to follow? Why?

3 Which set of notes do you think was fastest to write? Why?

The atomic bomb was developed by Albert Einstein, Leo Szeland and Enrico Fermi.

President Roosevelt set up research when America entered the war.

The bomb was developed in Oak Ridge, Tennessee.

The first nuclear explosion was at Los Alamos in New Mexico on 16 July 1945.

President Truman ordered the bomb's use to end the war with Japan.

The first bomb was dropped by Colonel Paul Tibbetts on Hiroshima on 6 August 1945.

Sally.

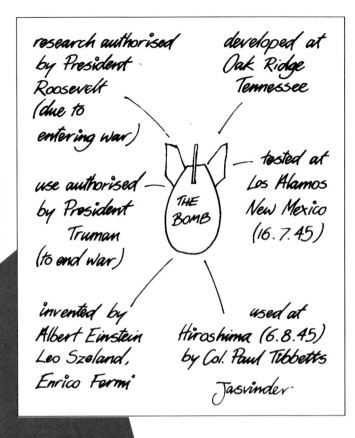

research authorised by President Roosevelt (due to entering war)

use authorised by President Truman (to end war)

invented by Albert Einstein Leo Szeland, Enrico Fermi

THE BOMB

developed at Oak Ridge Tennessee

tested at Los Alamos New Mexico (16.7.45)

used at Hiroshima (6.8.45) by Col. Paul Tibbetts

Jasvinder.

1 Inventors: Albert Einstein, Leo Szeland, Enrico Fermi
2 America into World War research (President Roosevelt agrees)
3 Site – Oak Ridge, Tennessee
4 1st bomb test – Los Alamos, New Mexico, 16 July 1945
5 1st use – Hiroshima, 6 August 1945, Colonel Paul Tibbetts)
    (authorised by President Truman to end war)

Malcolm

Making a selection

Writers, especially journalists, often have to select what they will report because they have more material than there is space for. If you needed to simplify these notes, which three details would you choose to leave out? Why?

Your turn

1 The next section of the history lesson, on page 140, explains the effects of the bomb on Hiroshima. Make notes from it for a friend who missed the lesson.
Think about the clearest way to set the notes out:
 • new points on new lines?
 • dividing it up into several parts?
 • underlining/highlighting the key points?
 • setting them out as a diagram?
Add ideas of your own as well.

2 When you have completed your notes, compare them with the notes made by another member of your group. What do you find helpful about each version?

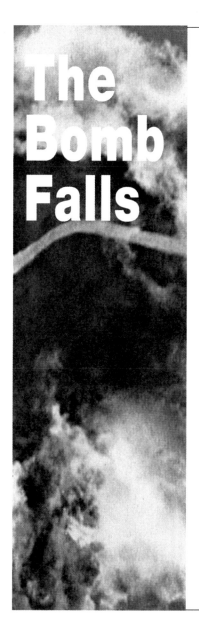

The Bomb Falls

One of the crew of the B29 which dropped the first atomic bomb, described how the world seemed to go purple when the bomb exploded. In the centre of Hiroshima itself, the explosion unleashed a ball of fire with a temperature of approximately 100 million degrees at its core. In this kind of heat, bodies simply disintegrated leaving no trace.

The fireball was followed by a wind that reached 500 miles per hour, uprooting trees and flattening buildings. The speed of the wind made things that were normally quite safe into dangerous missiles: people's skins were pierced even by blades of grass. One effect of the wind was to create a tidal wave which drowned thousands who were not killed by the blast.

In the longer term, the explosion resulted in a radiation sickness which has killed even more than the explosion itself did. During the weeks after the bomb fell, people found their skin affected by bleeding and their hair falling out. Thousands died of the sickness and many more who were less affected contracted cancer and were killed in that way.

The day of the bomb will never be forgotten by any who were involved. One eye witness said this: "I climbed on top of a pile of corpses. Layer upon layer of them. Some were still moving, still alive. I had to get over them. I can still hear the cracking of their bones."

Even the Americans, who had succeeded in their efforts, were taken aback. One airman, looking at the mushroom cloud with no idea about what had happened below it, said: "My God, what have we done?"

What is important?

The problem with making notes is often deciding exactly what is important. This will usually depend on what you need the notes for. A poet and a scientist might want to make very different notes about what happened at Hiroshima.

1 Divide your notes on the effects of the bomb into two sections, putting in the first section information that you believe is absolutely essential. For example:

Essential	Useful but not essential
fireball	10 million degrees

2 Compare your selection with that of a partner, concentrating particularly on the differences between your two choices.

3 Think about the differences between what would be considered important by these people and make brief notes about what they would be:
   • an historian
   • a doctor
   • a scientist
   • an anti-nuclear campaigner
   • a poet.

The question of what can happen when a bomb falls is dealt with vividly in Robert Swindells' novel **Brother on the land** and in Robert C O'Brien's **Z for Zachariah.**

Scientist

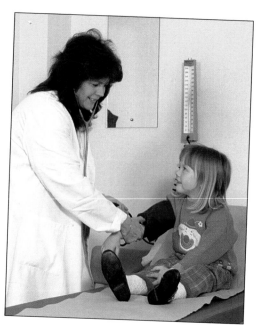

Doctor

CND Campaigner

SOLD ON IT

Information and persuasion

What would advertisers tell you if you asked them why they spend large sums of money on glossy magazine spreads or slick television commercials? Their answers would vary but they would almost certainly include some of the following reasons:

- to introduce a product
- to announce a product improvement
- to remind people about a product
- to re-assure people about a product.

Think about the advertisements that you have looked at recently.

1 What sort of people do you see in them?
2 What do the advertisements promise you?

What do you think?

Do you think that advertising affects you?
Does it influence what you buy?
Are other members of your family influenced by what they see advertised?

Selling your product

How would you present a new product to the public?

1 Look at the three product briefs.
2 Choose one of them.
3 Decide what you will call the new product.
4 Decide how and where you will advertise it.
5 Prepare your first advertisement(s) for a newspaper or magazine.
6 Prepare a *press release* – information on your new product that could be given to the press to tell them about it.

Reading advertisements: activities

Look at the four advertisements that follow. First of all, take a quick look as you would if you were flicking through a magazine or looking at a billboard. Then go back and look at each of the advertisements more closely:

- read the words carefully
- pick out any catchphrases or key messages
- look at the designs – think about the parts of the advertisements to which your eyes are drawn.

1 How did you respond to each advertisement?
2 How do you think each advert wants to make its readers feel?
3 What is the most important point being communicated in each advertisement?
4 Which instincts are being appealed to in each advertisement?
5 Which devices are being used to gain your attention?

> **HELP**
> Look at the diagrams on how advertisers work on pages 142 and 143 for help with questions 4 and 5.

PRODUCT BRIEFS

A A young people's magazine aimed at the 14 to 18 age group. It will focus on leisure activities and will include coverage of music, video, film and sport amongst its pages.

B A new soft drink aimed at the 11 to 14 age group with a dual emphasis on taste and health. The drink is being given a high vitamin and mineral content.

C An up-market chocolate bar with the emphasis on quality. This will be more expensive than its competitors but that may even be turned into an advantage by drawing attention to how good it tastes. It is hoped that the chocolate bar will appeal to young working adults with money to spend.

Power Money

Greed

 nostalgia: the idea that older is better.

"Standards"

technology: the idea that increased knowledge makes things better.

INSTINCTS TO WHICH AN
ADVERTISER MAY APPEAL

relationships

comfort

Getting on better

health

keeping up

having something that not many have yet discovered

being up with scientific advances

being in fashion

anything that makes
people go "aahh"
and smile

anything that makes
people laugh

DEVICES THAT AN
ADVERTISER MAY USE

images that make
people look
twice

scenes that look ideal and
make people want to be
a part of them

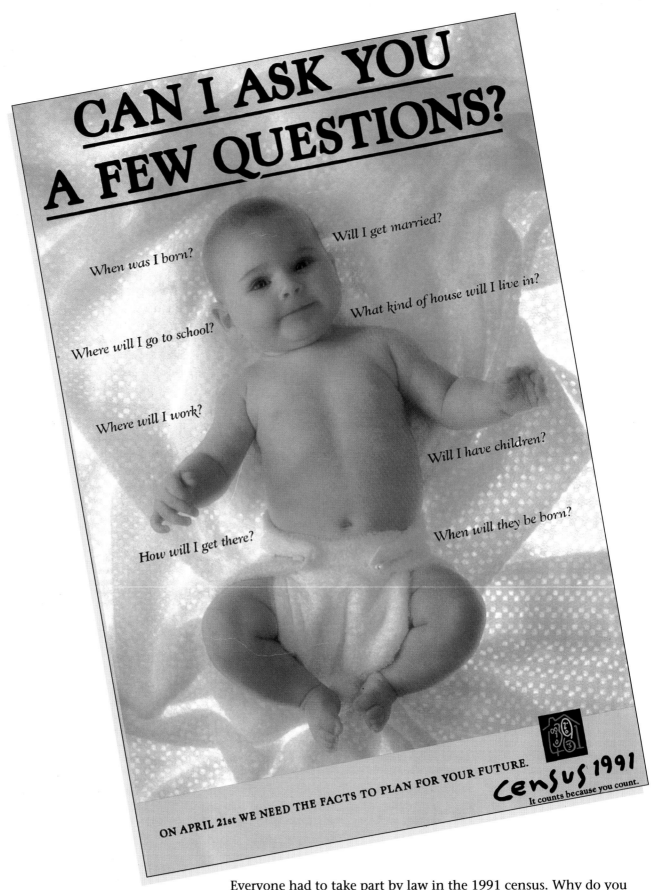

Everyone had to take part by law in the 1991 census. Why do you think the government bothered to spend money on advertising it?

For some of you this could be a Chamber of Horrors

However houseproud you are, dusting, vacuuming and cleaning will hardly disturb the numbers of the House Dust Mite, the unseen health-hazard that lives in every home, especially the bedroom.

House Dust Mites are microscopic creatures which live and multiply on the skin we shed, and they're found in large numbers in mattresses, soft furnishings and even cuddly toys.

For most people they're not a problem, but for Asthma or allergy sufferers, the House Dust Mite can be a serious threat.

The danger in your home

House Dust Mites produce powerful allergens which become airborne like pollen, to settle on and be inhaled by humans. These allergens are 'trigger' factors,

bringing on Asthma attacks, coughing, sneezing, runny noses and even Eczema, conditions which affect millions of people young and old.

Actomite destroys the invisible menace

Actomite is a new CFC-free spray which destroys House Dust Mites, their larvae and eggs.

Each application is an effective and long-lasting treatment which will protect an average sized room for up to 3 months, and is especially recommended for use in the bedroom.

If you want to save your family from the risks of sharing their bedrooms with the House Dust Mite, it makes sense to protect them with Actomite.

For further information please write to: Searle Consumer Products, PO Box 53, Lane End Road, High Wycombe, Buckinghamshire HP12 4HL.

ACTOMITE™
Actively Controls House Dust Mites

Available from Boots and all leading chemists.

Actomite is a trademark of G. D. Searle & Co

Searle Consumer Products
PO Box 53, Lane End Road, High Wycombe,
Buckinghamshire HP12 4HL.

The delicate aroma of truly fresh tea is completely protected.

HOW DO YOU KNOW YOU ENJOY FRESH TEA?

~

YOU'VE NOT TASTED IT YET.

IT'S NEW

TY·PHOO

EXTRA FRESH

EXTRA FRESH

Now discover the secret of truly fresh tea

The first brand to bring home the truly fresh taste of tea.

TEA BAGS

DISCOVER NEW TYPHOO EXTRA FRESH.

Until now there's been no really fresh tea for any of us to enjoy in the UK.

That's because all tea leaves lose their fresh taste as they travel.

But new Typhoo Extra Fresh is the first tea in history to pick and vacuum pack the tea leaves on the plantations.

The fresh flavour once captured then has Typhoo protection right up to the moment you take the tea bags out of the airtight foil pouches.

Try it and you'll discover Typhoo Extra Fresh has a fresh new taste all of its own.

TY·PHOO EXTRA FRESH 80 TEA BAGS

NOT JUST MAKING TEA ~ MAKING HISTORY

Many advertising agencies believe that photographs work far better than drawings. What do you think?

He's got the power. How about you?

This was one of the advertisements commissioned by the government when it was selling shares in two electricity generating companies, National Power and Powergen.

Further activities

1 What makes a good advertisement? From your study of the four advertisements and further ones of your choice, say what you think makes advertising work. Include advertisements cut from magazines and marked up to illustrate what you are saying.

2 A young person's guide to advertising. Write an article on advertising for an information book aimed at 12 to 13 year olds. Your article should include what advertising is, and the different types of advertising.

3 Making you want what you cannot afford? Write a magazine article that discusses the appeal of various advertisements and considers whether we are being encouraged to buy more than we should. You will need to collect examples from magazines to illustrate your points.

AMNESTY

Every advertiser needs to grab your attention. For organisations like Amnesty International who exist entirely on what people give them, advertising means survival.

Amnesty is not only a charity, it is a campaigning organisation that tries to see that governments treat people decently, that they give prisoners a fair trial and that they observe basic human rights. It works to combat torture and imprisonment without trial. It is also committed to the abolition of capital punishment. Not surprisingly, it is unpopular with most governments at some stages of its work.

The Amnesty Campaign

Look at the advertisement for Amnesty International.

1 What first catches your eye in this advertisement and makes you start reading?

2 Why do you think it is written as if the reader is the prisoner?

3 Why do you think the information is given in the form of a story?

4 Why do you think there is so much information in the story?

5 What is the purpose of the white square and the black square?

6 If you could afford to put this advertisement in only one newspaper, which would you choose? Why?

7 How would this advertisement persuade someone to give their support to Amnesty?

This square is white. By the time you reach the bottom of the page you'll agree or you'll be dead.

The square is of course black, but in certain countries that's not what's important. What matters is that you conform, and to make you conform the State has only one weapon. Fear.

Article 19 of The Universal Declaration of Human Rights states that everyone has the right to freedom of opinion and expression.

. You are one of the few prepared to speak out against the State. For a while, you appear to get away with it. But eventually they catch up with you. Initially it's just harassment, threats and phone calls. It's usually enough.

To continue to speak out against the State at this stage takes enormous courage.

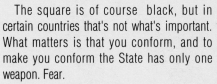

Your continued writings don't go unnoticed and this time they decide to arrest you. It is not the proverbial knock at the door at four in the morning; you're simply 'lifted' from the street in full public view. (It serves as a useful warning to anyone else who may be thinking the same dangerous thoughts.)

Article 9 states that no-one shall be subjected to arbitrary arrest.

You're held for a week or so in solitary, you're not sure exactly how long. Your only visitors are the prison guards who seem free to beat you whenever they choose. You're deprived of water, food and sleep; and are surprised when, after a final beating, you're thrown into the street.

You know that from now on your life, and the lives of your family and friends will be in constant danger.

What colour is the square?

It seems incredible that there are individuals who, in the face of enormous personal risk, are yet prepared to campaign against the most barbaric regimes. Your struggle continues.

Now you try to hide your actions, holding secret meetings and writing under assumed names. But you are already very well known to the authorities and naturally they don't need evidence for your subsequent re-arrest. Indeed they don't need any for your trial. You don't get one.

Article 10 states that everyone is entitled...to a fair and public hearing.

The State has finally lost patience with you. You've disappeared. Your family don't know whether you're alive or dead. You no longer exist.

What colour is the square?

But you are still alive; just. Your body is a map of fresh scar tissue and electrical burns. Your one meal a day is rancid. It's too dark to remove all the insects from it. Despite horrific injuries your torture continues.

It seems your activities were having some effect outside. The only reason you are still alive is that you have names and information that the State wants.

Article 5 states that no-one shall be subjected to torture.

To have your fingernails torn out or the soles of your feet beaten is merely to be softened up in an age where methods of torture are as varied as they are hideous. The gruesome reality is that few survive unless they surerrender the information sought.

You've come face to face with man at his most evil. You're at the mercy of State functionaries prepared to commit in describable atrocities. Yet your only crime was to have an opinion that ran contrary to that of the State and to share it with your friends.

Now your only possible escape is to give their names to your torturers: to subject them to all that you have endured.

Even if you do that you still have no guarantee that your torture will cease or that you will ever be released. If you remain silent, you will die. The choice is *yours*.

What colour is the square?

Article 1 states that all human beings are born free and equal in dignity and rights.

Since 1961 Amnesty International have striven to advance the cause of human rights throughout the world.

They have always relied entirely on voluntary contributions.

Amnesty membership costs £5, but please send whatever you can afford to: Amnesty International, 99-119 Rosebery Avenue, London EC1R 4RE.

AMNESTY INTERNATIONAL

Making AMNESTY INTERNATIONAL *known*

The advertisement you have been looking at was targeted at adults. Now create an advertisement for Amnesty aimed at students in your school or college. This can be planned as a wall display or as a spread in a school magazine. Assume that your readers know nothing about the organisation.

1 First gather the information you need about Amnesty International from the following extracts and articles. They have been organised under four headings:
   • What is Amnesty International?
   • Why does it need to help...who does it need to help?
   • How does it work?
   • Some success stories.
   Make brief notes for yourself under these headings so that you form your own information dossier.

2 Now decide what angle you are going to take in your advertisement and what material you will use. *You will not be able to cram in everything from your dossier and still expect to interest the casual reader.* Some possible approaches are:
   • Looking at it from one point of view such as that of an Amnesty volunteer, a prison guard or the child of a prisoner.
      • Taking several stories to give a fuller idea of what Amnesty International achieves.
      • Concentrating on the problems that Amnesty exists to fight.
   These are only suggestions – try to come up with ideas of your own.

3 Prepare your advertisement. Think about:
   • attracting and holding the readers' attention
   • arousing their sympathy
   • using language and a style which will appeal to them.

What is Amnesty International?

Amnesty International is a worldwide human rights movement which works impartially for the release of prisoners of conscience: men, women and children detained anywhere for their beliefs, colour, ethnic origin, sex, religion or language, provided they have neither used nor advocated the use of violence.   Amnesty International opposes torture and the death penalty in all cases without reservation and advocates fair and prompt trials for all political prisoners. Amnesty International is independent of all governments, political factions, ideologies, economic interests and religious creeds.

SOME FACTS:

◆ Over 700,000 members and supporters in over 150 countries.

◆ Since 1961 Amnesty has adopted or investigated more than 34,000 Prisoners of Conscience. Of these, over 29,000 cases are now closed.

◆ 1989 Amnesty began work on 1,143 new cases.

◆ 1,062 prisoners were released in 1989.

◆ In 1989, Amnesty sent 67 missions to 37 countries.

◆ In the first 11 months of 1989 Amnesty learned of over 1,900 executions.

Why does it need to help...
who does it need to help?

◆ In more than 50 countries you can be imprisoned without charge or trial. Sometimes for years.

◆ Torture is reported as a systematic part of the interrogation process in over 60 countries.

◆ More than half the countries of the world still have the death penalty, often for political offences not involving violence.

◆ Since 1961 there have been tens of thousands of "disappearances". Victims often vanish after being taken into custody.

CASE STUDIES

In **Brazil** three-year old Clésio was shot in the back while riding on his father's shoulders. The killers then shot the father, a simple peasant, at point blank range in the head. His widow, who had witnessed the killings, was reportedly told by the local police chief that he could not register the crime as he had no pen or paper!

Thousands of members of the Brazani community "disappeared" after their arrest in **Iraq**. Among them were 300 children aged between 8 and 17. Nothing has been heard of them in six years.

Noor Jahan was 1 year old when arrested with her mother in **Burma**. Now, aged 32, she and her mother have at last been released.

In the **USA** 27 young people are under sentence of death – for crimes committed when they were under 18.

How does it work?

WHAT YOU CAN ACHIEVE BY SIMPLY WRITING A LETTER

Our URGENT ACTION scheme is one of our most successful ways of campaigning against injustice. When we hear about a detainee needing immediate help, we set out to get all the facts.

We depend on meticulous research into allegations of human rights violations. We put great importance on impartial reporting.

When the facts are verified they go out within hours to our URGENT ACTION network. Around the globe, 30,000 people send letters and cables to government authorities to plead the case of individual prisoners. Last year we ran URGENT ACTION appeals on behalf of 2,886 individuals in 87 countries.

How effective are they? In 40% of cases the prisoner's condition improves. Torture stops...the prisoner sees a doctor or a lawyer...or is taken out of solitary confinement. A former torturer in El Salvador has said that these appeals can make the difference between life and death:

"If there's an appeal from a foreign government or Amnesty International they will live. Otherwise, they are dead." Sending a letter overseas is an inexpensive way to help a prisoner. And the results can be dramatic. This is what happened to a union leader who was being kept naked in an underground cell in the Dominican Republic:

"When the first 200 letters came, the guards gave me back my clothes. The next 200 letters came and the prison officers came to see me.

When the next pile of letters arrived, the director got in touch with his superior. The letters kept coming, 3,000 of them, and the President called the prison and told them to let me go.

After I was released, the President called me to his office for a man-to-man talk. He said: "How is it that a trade union leader like you has so many friends all over the world? He showed me an enormous box of letters he had received, and when we parted he gave them to me."

Some success stories

THE MAGIC FOOTBALL

Letting prisoners know they aren't forgotten does wonders for their morale. When a Liverpool group discovered their adopted prisoner in Cameroon was a soccer fan they sent him a football signed by the Liverpool team! It worked like magic: it cheered up the prisoner...and the guards treated him better.

part of a 'thank you' letter from a freed Paraguayan prisoner

After world-wide appeals, this little boy and his mother are finally free – unlike thousands who have 'disappeared' or been killed. The mother, a journalist in El Salvador, endured two and a half years as a Prisoner of Conscience. There were fears that her son would be killed by the death squads – so he was hidden indoors by his grandmother. "I'm so happy to be free," he says, "I could kiss everybody."

On Christmas Eve the door of my cell opened and the guard tossed in a crumpled piece of paper. It said: 'Take heart. the world knows you are alive.' That letter saved my life.

MAY 9TH

This unit looks at how newspapers present themselves by the way they use their front pages and the way they approach a major story.

What am I buying it for?

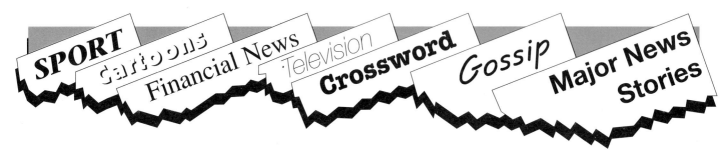

Make a list of the parts of a newspaper you would turn to if you bought one or there was one in the house. Try to list them in order of importance to you.

Front page appeal

Look at the following three front pages and answer the following questions:

1 What major differences can you see between the three front pages?

2 In what ways are they similar?

3 What do you think is the strength of each front page?

4 What do you think the front pages tell you about the readers of each newspaper?

advertising what is inside

picture to re-inforce headline

bold headlines

makes it sound as if she personally wrote it

See page 2

the single story front page

Why advertise the number of pages?

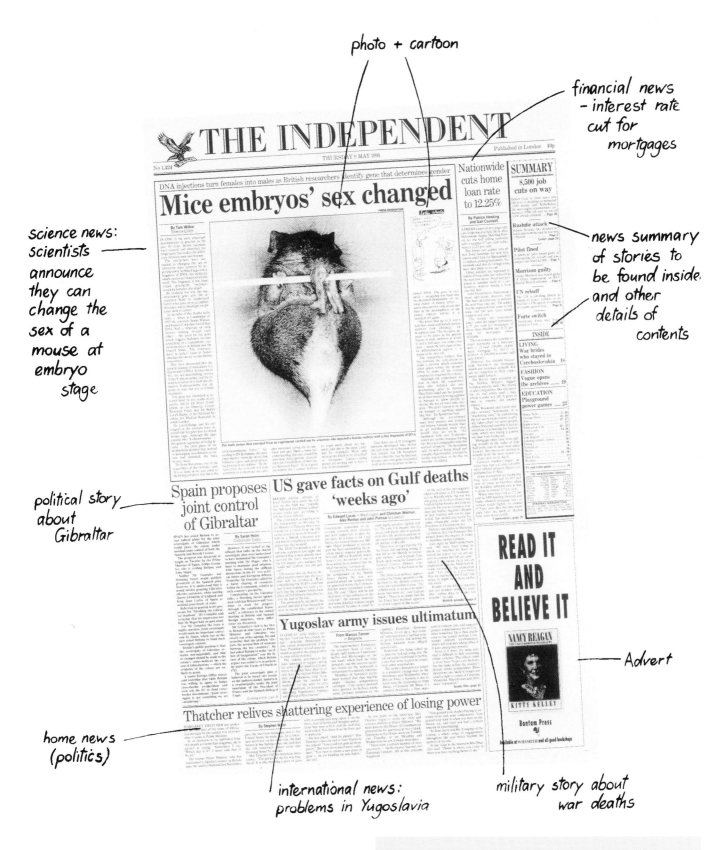

photo + cartoon

financial news - interest rate cut for mortgages

science news: scientists announce they can change the sex of a mouse at embryo stage

news summary of stories to be found inside, and other details of contents

political story about Gibraltar

home news (politics)

international news: problems in Yugoslavia

military story about war deaths

Advert

Why have so many stories on the front page?

Inside story about a celebrity

Today

25p (Republic of Ireland 36p)

★ ★ ★ ★

My Rags to Riches Story

MICHAEL ASPEL WRITES AS HE'S NEVER WRITTEN BEFORE PAGE 19

Debris of my shattered life, by Maggie Thatcher

by PAUL WILENIUS
Political Editor

A BITTER Mrs Thatcher has opened her heart and talked for the first time of how her life was shattered when she was "bundled out" of office.

In the most emotional interview she has given since being replaced as Premier, she said her entire world was smashed like a pane of glass dropped on the floor.

Now she is finding it impossible to pick up the pieces.

The deeply moving account of how she was betrayed will appear in June's issue of Vanity Fair magazine.

"The pattern of my life was fractured," she said. "It is like throwing a pane of glass with a complicated map upon it on the floor, and all habits and thoughts and actions that went with it, and the staff that went with it. You threw it on the floor and it shattered."

Blazed

Writer Maureen Orth asked: "And the pieces?"

Mrs Thatcher's eyes blazed as she replied: "You could not pick up those pieces."

In effect, she was "bundled out", Mrs Thatcher said, and forced to pack up and vacate Number 10 and Chequers on just four days' notice. She never wants this ever to happen to a future leader.

She said angrily: "I will suggest that no future prime minister has to do that, because prime ministers have a dignity as ex-prime ministers by virtue of their office."

Mrs Thatcher refused to consider the poll tax as an error.

And if the people had been given the chance, she said, they would have given her a historic fourth General Election victory.

Miss Orth said Mrs Thatcher cut a strangely poignant figure, unable fully to come to terms with the disaster that hit her.

Five times during the interview Mrs Thatcher said: "I have never been defeated by the people."

She added: "I have never been
Turn to Page 6

has the attraction of fear/horror

THIS DOG DESTROYED FRANK TEMPEST'S FACE IN 30 MINUTES OF BLOODY SAVAGERY
..and the law does nothing

campaigning stance

by RICHARD CREASY and ROB PERKINS

BAKER Frank Tempest was last night lying in a hospital bed, his face mutilated beyond recognition after being savaged by two American pit bull terriers.

The father-of-four was a few feet from his front door when the pets leapt over a 7ft fence and dragged him screaming into the gutter. For 30 terrifying minutes the dogs tore at his face and body. Police marksmen later shot one dead. The other was captured and put down.

Last night, as MPs demanded a ban on imported fighting dogs, officers admitted: "We can't take the owner to court. The dogs have been destroyed and there's not a lot more we can do." Mr Tempest, 54, was walking home from work at the local bakery in Lincoln when he was attacked at 5.30am.

Witness Malcolm Sandy said: "They were pulling him along the street. He was being bitten from head to toe – it was horrifying."

Mr Tempest was rescued by a passer-who beat the animals off with a stick. He was rushed to Leicester Royal Infirmary where surgeons spent six hours rebuilding his face.

"I've never seen such severe injuries," said
Turn to Page 5

Turn to page 6

Turn to page 5

politics + personality interest

This is the only paper which puts the dog attack on the front page. Think of a reason for giving the story front page status.

Same story, different reports

The one story on all three front pages was the ex prime minister's interview about her downfall. Here is the first part of the report in each of the papers together with the headline.

1 What differences do you notice in the reporting?

2 Which report is most sympathetic to the ex-leader and which is least sympathetic? What words or phrases give you evidence for your views?

Debris of my shattered life, by Maggie Thatcher

by PAUL WILENIUS
Political Editor

A BITTER Mrs Thatcher has opened her heart and talked for the first time of how her life was shattered when she was 'bundled out' of office.

In the most emotional interview she has given since being replaced as Premier, she said her entire world was smashed like a pane of glass dropped on the floor.

Now she is finding it impossible to pick up the pieces.

The deeply moving account of how she was betrayed will appear in June's issue of Vanity Fair magazine.

"The pattern of my life was fractured," she said. "It is like throwing a pane of glass with a complicated map upon it on the floor, and all habits and thoughts and actions that went with it, and the staff that went with it. You threw it on the floor and it shattered."

from Today

Thatcher relives shattering experience of losing power

Margaret Thatcher has spoken for the first time of the sense of dislocation wrought by

By Stephen Ward

the sudden loss of power after 11 years as Prime Minister.

In an interview to be published later this month in *Vanity Fair* magazine, she is quoted as saying: "Sometimes I say, 'Which day is it?' I never said that at No 10."

The former Prime Minister, who has maintained a dignified reserve in Britain since her sudden dismissal last November, gave the interview during her visit to the United States six weeks ago. In a television interview on the same visit, she had hinted at her feelings when she said that she still sometimes almost turns into Downing Street by mistake.

Mrs Thatcher told her American interviewer: "The pattern of my life was fractured. It is like throwing a pane of glass with a complicated map upon it on the floor. And all habits and thoughts and actions that went with it, and the staff that went with it. You threw it on the floor and it shattered."

from The Independent

158 MAY 9TH

I'M SHATTERED

The anguish of being bundled out of No 10.

Bitter Margaret Thatcher has spoken out for the first time of her anger and despair at being "bundled out" of 10 Downing Street.

In a remarkable interview made public yesterday, the ousted Premier confessed that last November's Tory revolt left her shattered.

No future Prime Minister should have to face the same humiliation, she said.

The "disoriented" ex-Premier told the interviewer:

"Sometimes I say 'Which day is it?' I never said that at No 10."

And the woman who embraced "family values" made this astonishing admission: "Home is where you come when you have nothing better to do." Mrs Thatcher went on to speak of:

Her DOWNFALL. "The pattern of my life was fractured. It is like throwing a pane of glass with a complicated map on the floor.

"You threw it on the floor and it shattered... You could not pick up the pieces."

from the Daily Mirror

Writing about newspapers

Look carefully at the contents of two different newspapers over several days. Write a report for your group on the similarities and the differences between them. Among the things you might look at are:

- space given to national and international news
- space given to particular interests such as sport, finance, fashion
- amount of advertising and type of advertising
- the way that the same subjects are treated
- the political bias (or lack of it)
- the use of photographs
- who the paper might appeal to.

TORMENTED CHIMPS:
A MATTER OF OPINION

Most of what we read in the press is a complicated mixture of fact and opinion, and it is not always easy to distinguish one from the other.

Fact and opinion

1 Read the article opposite.

2 Now sift through the article a second time, trying to sort known fact from speculation or opinion.
This needs a lot of care. For example, the opening paragraph of the article contains the following fact/opinion mix:
Facts – four chimpanzees spent the night in an animal sanctuary. Unless the article is a complete fabrication no-one can doubt this.
Opinions – "life of hell", "pawns in a money-spinning tourist game". As they stand, such statements have not been supported by evidence, they are opinions rather than hard facts.

Loaded language

There is also a *grey area* between self-evident fact and obvious opinion. The words "recovering" and "safety" are examples of this. The chimps might be "recovering" from something, they might not be; the animal sanctuary might be "safe", it might not be. This use of *loaded language* needs careful consideration, as it can often suggest something to a reader without needing to prove it. Work through the article again paragraph by paragraph listing:

- all the statements you consider to be incontrovertible facts
- the statements, words or phrases which you understand to be clear expressions of opinion
- loaded language, in between fact and opinion, which suggests without proving anything.

When you have finished, discuss your findings with others in your group.

Right of reply

Finally, whatever you might think of using animals in this way, allow the restaurant owner, Antonio Vacas, a right of reply. Write the letter he would send in response to the article, where he replies to some of the arguments used and defends using chimpanzees as photographic props.

SPAIN CRACKS DOWN ON ANIMAL CRUELTY THAT SHAMES ITS TOURIST TRADE

GETTING TOUGH: A photographer arrives to plead with police for his chimp and officers start their raids backed by Jim Cronin, above

Tormented chimps are free at last

From JO REVILL
in Gran Canaria
Pictures: KEITH PANNELL

SICK: Crippled chimp Kyko in the rescuers' cage and, left, the creature dressed up for a snap with diners

FOUR chimpanzees were recovering in the safety of an animal sanctuary last night, rescued from a life of hell as pawns in a money-spinning tourist game.

They are the first to be snatched to freedom as Spain cracks down on a sickening trade which sees them drugged, starved, humiliated and used as toys on holiday beaches.

The Canary Islands are spearheading a new move in Spain to act on international agreements banning photographers from using animals as living props.

Pressure

Last week I took part in the first raids of the blitz.

For years, holidaymakers have been revolted by the way the animals are hawked round restaurants and seashores.

Under growing tourist pressure the Spaniards finally decided they had to take action.

In a series of raids, customs officers and police worked side by side to seize chimps Kyko, Mona, Rocky and Mojo from bars and private addresses around Gran Canaria, an island normally packed with Britons.

Four-year-old male Kyko and the others will taste freedom at last in a Dorset sanctuary owned by New Yorker Jim Cronin.

The pitiful creature can no longer walk after spending most of his short life on roller skates, scooting round to amuse diners at Antonio Vacas's restaurant.

After two hours of frustrated argument officers from Spain's national police force, the Guardia Civil, throw Vacas into the back of their van and charge him with 'being uncooperative', which means an instant spell in prison.

The same afternoon a magistrate is summoned and the chimp is finally handed over.

Jim had spent three years pleading with the Spanish authorities to take action.

After last week's rescue missions he looked at the four animals in his care and said: 'I never thought this moment would come because Spain seemed so backward in its approach to wildlife.

'In a few years the beaches might be free of the gross spectacle of chimps, dressed up and drugged up for tourists.'

Blinded

The raids began at 11.30am last Tuesday. When the command 'Vamos!' is given a convoy of jeeps, cars and motorbikes rolls down the streets of Maspalomas in the south of Gran Canaria.

The officers thump on the door of a dirty stone building and out comes a dishevelled man with straggly hair and torn shirt. He rubs his eyes and gabbles furiously at our party — six police, four customs officers, two vets, Jim and ourselves.

Then a one-armed beach photographer arrived to plead for the release of one chimp, Charlie,

In his back yard we see the remains of chicken legs and chips, the only nourishment for Mona, living in a crate two feet wide and three feet high.

The ape has been turned into a junkie by her owner, who likes her subdued when she is thrust into the arms of tourists.

She has also had her teeth pulled out and is almost blinded by cataracts after four years living on left-overs.

After much pleading Mona is handed over and put gently into one of Jim's crates.

As he and I pick it up, an unexpected wave of emotion floods over me. I realise we are both grinning like idiots.

'This is what success feels like,' he says delightedly in his Bronx drawl. 'After three years of hassling, I have my baby.'

Another chimp has been brought into the Guardia station and the three are chattering away in a police garage.

Jim has invited over a British vet, John Lewis, to oversee the animals' health and he is putting sedation tablets into bananas to calm them down.

who was clearly ill. He said the ape was nine, in good health and his best friend. The authorities gave him the creature back after the man promised not to use him any more for photographs.

Three other seizures were similarly thwarted.

One of the guardia spat in disgust.

'A British tourist had a row last year with a photographer,' he said. 'Then the guy called his mates and they chased the tourist, who jumped over a balcony to escape. He broke nearly every bone in his body and was lucky to survive.'

Woodland

An owner can be charged with illegal possession, but if he has papers to show the animal was bought more than five years ago it might be contested.

For CITES, the international rules on trade in endangered species which make it illegal to own a chimp, came into force only in 1986.

The four chimps we rescued were almost certainly taken from their mothers killed by trappers in the jungle.

Organised gangs will have put them on to boats to Las Palmas

from Equatorial Guinea or Senegal.

They will then have been taken to dealers working from home.

With our cargo of four animals, enjoying an occasional bottle of Coke which they love, we made our way through the night to Las Palmas airport where they were loaded on to a plane for Barcelona.

They are staying at an animal sanctuary there, run by Britons Simon and Peggy Templar, until the paperwork is sorted out for their new home in England.

Jim is sure they will adapt perfectly well to their natural surroundings in woodland at his Dorset sanctuary. 'I have watched my animals learning to be chimps again,' he said, feeding Rocky a banana.

As we left Gran Granaria, the Guardia Civil team all wanted to shake Jim's hand and assure him the first four apes were just the start.

'We are with you,' they said, simply.

● Anyone with information about beach chimps should contact Jim Cronin at Monkey World Chimp Rescue Centre, Longthorne, East Stoke, Wareham, Dorset BH20 6HH.

STEREOTYPED

From our fingerprints to our genes, everybody is an individual: there is no one anywhere in the world quite like you. However, everybody fits into at least some groups as well – student, rugby player, ballet dancer, Scotsman, train spotter, wheelchair user...

A stereotype is somebody who is considered to represent a particular group. That need not be a bad thing if the description helps us to understand the group. However many descriptions of groups have become oversimplified and negative in the course of time. For example, students are often pictured as lazy and keen to live off the money earned by people who do "real" work. Although this might be true of a particular individual, it is very unfair to suggest that all students are like that.

What stereotypes can you come up with for the other five groups mentioned – rugby player, ballet dancer, Scotsman, train spotter, wheelchair user? Which of these stereotypes would be most damaging to the people involved?

To look at stereotyping means to look at what people expect of other people. The way we stereotype people often reveals more about our prejudices than it does about the people being stereotyped. This unit concentrates mainly on the differences between what is expected of boys or men and of girls or women.

Robert Geary

Look at the four people pictured on this page. What would you have done in their situation?

1

"Everyone thinks that I will be intelligent because I wear glasses. Then they moan because I can't do the work."

2

"The sports teacher cannot believe that I am useless at running. He didn't say that it was because I'm tall and black but I know that's what was going through his head."

3

"My dad simply refuses to take me to matches. He'd take Paul but Paul doesn't even watch it on television."

4

"When I chose Textiles and the Food option in Technology everyone laughed so much that I changed my options. Now I'm doing some subjects I don't even like."

MEET THE McKENZIES

WHO'S WHO?

Nancy McKenzie – left school at 15 and went to work in a baker's shop. She married at 18 and had Mick soon after. Then came Mandy and later the twins. At present Nancy has a part-time job in a factory making window frames and is studying for A-level Economics at the local tech.

Mick – left school at 16 and now works in a record shop. He plays lead guitar in a local group and dreams about 'breaking into the big time'. He spends most of what he earns on music and making himself look good.

Reg McKenzie – got an apprenticeship when he left school and qualified as a car mechanic. He's worked for the same garage for the last 17 years and is now the senior mechanic in one of the two main repair shops. He is a committed union man and his great passion is football.

Sharon and Garry – Four-year-old twins due to start school at Easter. They get looked after by their Gran four mornings a week while Nancy goes to work, and on Friday she takes them to a local play group, while Nancy goes to college.

Mandy – is still at school with two years to go before taking her exams. She likes school most of the time – mainly because she's good at sport and plays in the school netball, hockey, tennis and athletics teams. She often gets fed-up with the way boys and girls are treated differently at school and has a reputation for being a bit 'outspoken' on the matter.

Scenes from family life...

Expectations

1 What do you think is Reg Mckenzie's attitude to women?

2 What other stereotypes can you see in what the characters say and do?

3 How might the twins be influenced by stereotypes as they grow up in this environment?

4 Which character makes you most annoyed? Why?

5 With which character do you have most sympathy? Why?

6 Produce a chart that shows what you think is expected of the different sexes. It might start like this:

Girls/Women	Boys/Men
CAN COOK	*CAN MOW THE LAWN*

Speaking out

Develop one of the scenes suggested by the cartoons into a full-blown argument between two or more characters. Your scene might not be the one shown in the cartoon but one that happens afterwards for example, an argument between Nancy McKenzie and her neighbour about mothers going to college. If you set out your argument as a playscript, you can check your layout by looking at pages 80 and 81.

Men Talk

Women
Rabbit rabbit rabbit women
Tattle and titter
Women prattle
Women waffle and witter

Men talk. Men talk.

Women into Girl Talk
About Women's Trouble
Trivia 'n' Small Talk
They yap and they babble

Men Talk. Men Talk.

Women yatter
Women chatter
Women chew the fat, women spill the beans
Women aint been takin'
The oh-so Good Advice in them
Women's Magazines

A Man Likes A Good Listener

Oh yeah
I like a Woman
Who likes me enough
Not to nitpick
Not to nag and
Not to interrupt 'cause I call that treason
A woman with the Good Grace
To be struck dumb
By me Sweet Reason. Yes –
A Man Likes a Good Listener

A real
Man
Likes a Real Good Listener

Women yap yap yap
Verbal Diarrhoea is a Female Disease
Woman she spread she rumours round she
Like Philadelphia Cream Cheese.

Oh
Bossy Women Gossip
Girlish Women Giggle
Women natter, women nag
Women niggle niggle niggle
Men Talk.

Men
Think first, Speak Later
Men Talk.

Liz Lochhead

Performance

1 In your group discuss how you would perform this poem to bring out the bias and the prejudice that Liz Lochhead is writing about. Think about:
   - the way you will show the differences between the verses
   - the effect of the extra capital letters
   - how you will say the colloquial terms such as "yatter" and "prattle"
   - accents you might use.

2 Read it aloud and try out some of your ideas.

3 Perform your version for the rest of the class.

Loaded words

Liz Lochhead's poem is full of words which describe talking but are loaded with negative associations.
- Pick out five of them.
- Say not only what the word means but also what it is about the word that creates the negative sense. For example, *prattle* means to talk quickly. It is often used about babies talking, so it also gives an impression of childish or meaningless speech.
- Say why she uses these words.

Talking about young people

When adults talk about young people, they sometimes lapse into a similar kind of prejudice based on stereotypes. What negative words and phrases with negative associations can you think of that an unsympathetic adult might use about young people. For example:

FOUL-MOUTHED   LOUD   IDLE   LAYABOUT   GOOD-FOR-NOTHING   IGNORANT

Produce a conversation between two adults about young people. The adults could be talking across a garden fence, in a bar, on a park bench...the choice is up to you. The conversation could include stereotypes of:

- the music young people listen to
- the amount of work they do
- the way they speak

- the way they dress
- the way they spend their time
- their attitudes to adults.

SOUNDING OFF

Stereotyping is the ploy of cowards, and labelling kills the spirit. Include me out, says Maya Angelou, best selling author and Hollywood's first black woman director.

WHY MAYA ANGELOU WON'T BE STEREOTYPED

Everybody is stereotyped: the bank managers, the Lord Plushbottom, the actor and actress, the pregnant woman, the Black, the Asian, the White. And that's because we're all so blitheringly ignorant. People hope that by tagging or labelling a person they won't have to consider if that person loves spring flowers, or is frightened of the dark, or longs for Christmas. You put on the label and that's all the person is.

I was standing in a queue at an airport not too long ago at the Hertz car rental desk. There were maybe about fifteen people and I may have been the fifth in line. All the rest of the people were white. A woman came along looking at this incredible line and after she sized everybody up she stood in front of me. So I tapped the man who had been in front of me all along and asked, "Is she with you?" and the man said, "No

madam." And I said, "Listen lady, find yourself some place and sit down. Don't get on a bus, don't get on a streetcar, don't get in a taxi and for God's sake don't get on an aeroplane. Of all the people in this line to come and get in front of, you chose me. That tells me you have bad luck all over you."

It's been my fortune to not suffer fools gladly. In fact I really don't suffer them at all, regardless of age, sex, race, position, profession. Nobody slides. I know that what the stereotype means to do is to kill the person, kill the spirit, kill the ambition, kill the hope, kill the desire, kill the aspirations, kill the growth, kill the breadth and I will *not* have that happen to me.

I think stereotypes are made for a number of reasons. One is the desire for power and control over those who are stereotyped. It's also the

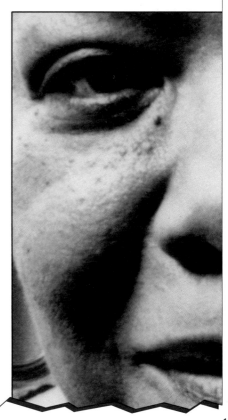

action of a lazy person: "I don't want to hear it, right?" Don't tell me. This is how it's always been. It is also the ploy of a coward: "I've got mine, don't try to encroach, stay away."

And, of course, the person who is the victim of the stereotyping is not expected to move beyond those boundaries set for him or her. Now in some cases the stereotyping acts as an ignition and turns the person into a whirling dervish who says, 'The hell you say I can't do that. You wanna bet? Who made that rule? We'll see,' and sets about to refute, to shatter the walls meant to imprison him or her. But for the most part the initiator and the object are both bruised. If they are bruised then life itself, the quality of life, is lessened. For instance, can you imagine what would happen in Britain if all the wit, the vitality, the humour, the creativity and the endurance of black people were integrated into British life? Can you imagine?

My great-grandma had been born a slave. Nobody knows where she came from. She was illiterate but she had named her daughters Annie, Elma, Ida, Ola and Ulla. Somehow she'd heard about the vowels. Then she got a job in a white Methodist church in Magnolia, Arkansas as a sacristan so that these five black girls in 1890 were able to get some education. She named herself Kentucky Shannon and when she was asked why, she said she liked the sound of it. My grandma was her eldest daughter. At the turn of the century my grandmother was married. The marriage didn't work. It was around 1903 and my grandmother got a divorce. Now that was unheard of. *White* women didn't get divorced.

There was a cotton gin on one side of town and a lumber mill on the other side, miles away. On Monday mornings my grandmother would take her brazier and stand in front of the lumber mill and start to fry pies. When the lunch bell rang the men would come out and buy the pies hot for five cents. Any she didn't sell she would wrap in a tea towel and, leaving her two sons in the care of someone, she would run across town to the cotton gin and sell these lukewarm pies for three cents. Then on Tuesday she would be in front of the cotton gin and sell them hot for five cents. And finally she developed such a clientele that she built herself a stall right in between the two, so the *men* could run to her at lunchtime. This was a woman who had been born to a person who had been a slave, a black woman who said, 'Stereotypes – no, not me. Include me out.'

My mother was the first black woman

radio operator in the navy and retired in 1980. She said this to me on several occasions: "Whenever you are in a threatening situation use all your energy to be present in it. People can turn into mobs in seconds if you withdraw, tear you limb from limb." Some people, they just go inside themselves and I'm sorry to say they let themselves be beaten, either physically or psychologically. And so they are stereotyped and minimised.

I'm the first black female director in Hollywood. I'm on the board of trustees of the American Film Institute. I am Reynolds Professor at Wake Forest University in North Carolina – a lifetime appointment. I'm Distinguished Visiting Professor at Radcliffe University. I have about 35 honorary doctorates. I teach in Spanish and French. I have a grandson and a son. I co-produced a film a few years ago called *Sisters* which represented the first time any studio or network had risked $1.5 million in a black woman's hands. I write songs – one was in the top ten for Roberta Flack.

I love life but I'm not in love with it. I will not live at *any* cost and that liberates me from anybody's attempt to belittle or stereotype me. Every person is worthy to live his or her life with as much dignity and laughter and wit and love and health as possible, no greater, no lesser than any other human being. I don't know how people get the idea that because this one is taller, whiter, fatter, he's more worthy to live life. Baloney.

Looking at the article

1 What does Maya Angelou say stereotyping is?

2 How has Maya Angelou been a victim of stereotyping and how has she challenged it?

3 How did her mother and grandmother challenge it in their own time?

4 What impression do you get of Maya Angelou from your reading?
   • Try to describe both her character and her beliefs.
   • What evidence can you find to support your impressions?

Extensions

1 School and stereotypes

All schools hope to do the best for their students and most believe they offer equal opportunities to everyone. What happens in your school? You might look at:
• option choices
• sporting opportunities
• work experience opportunities
• who occupies positions of authority in the school
• the occasions when the sexes are separated and the reasons.
What do the staff think?
What do the pupils think?

2 Challenging stereotypes: a personal essay

Write a personal essay of your own on stereotypes. Decide who you are writing for. For example:
• my dad because he believes women are useless and he has no idea how angry and frustrated he can make me feel
• my aunt because she is on the council and I think she could do more to change things if she understood more about how people feel
• people at the youth club because there are a lot of people there who will just go along with what anyone else tells them
• primary school teachers because they have so much influence on the way you think for the rest of your life.

3 What goes into the making of a stereotype? You can write about this in any way that you wish but one way would be to present it as a recipe. For example:

Take one pound of prejudice

Split this into equal parts for each. . .

What Stereotypes?

male/female

black/white

young/old

city/country

rich/poor

COUCH POTATOES
OR ACTIVE VIEWERS?

A DEBATE AMONGST EXPERTS

Is television a good or bad thing, especially for young people? The extracts quoted here present the arguments on both sides of the case.

1 Read through the materials carefully and discuss them in small groups. Identify the main points made on both sides.

2 What evidence is used to support these points of view?

3 What do you think? Base your answer both on the arguments given here and your own experience of television. This is a subject where every one of us has expert knowledge.

Couch potatoes...?

In California there is a group called the Couch Potatoes, who consider themselves "the true televisionaries". They take their name from their favourite place for vegetating, in front of the television set, and from a vegetable with many eyes. An advertisement to recruit members for the group goes like this:

"Do you enjoy excessive amounts of TV viewing? Were some of the most enjoyable times of your life experienced in front of your set? Were your formative years nurtured by the 'electronic babysitter'? Are you annoyed by crybaby intellectuals who claim that TV viewing is counterproductive and a waste of time? Like to do most of your living on a couch?" Asked by a reporter to comment on a two-way cable TV system that allows viewers to talk back to television, one of the Couch Potatoes responded: "Why watch TV if you have to think and respond? As far as I'm concerned, the main point of watching TV is that it lets you avoid having to

do that. To put it another way, if you're going to have to respond to your TV, you might as well go out and cultivate friendships or read a book or something."

Patricia Marks Greenfield *Mind and Media*

...or active viewers?

*T*elevision is part of growing up, probably quite an important part; often, a beneficial part, which we have hardly begun to take seriously, so busy are we looking for the 'bad effects' and for something other than ourselves to blame for the cruelty and selfishness in our society.

I have argued that television serves many useful purposes for children. It informs them; it helps to structure their lives; it gives them common interests with their friends and with other members of the family; it provides an occasion for family togetherness, discussion and sometimes argument. It gives them ideas for play and work; it can be used and studied at school.

Above all, children use television primarily as entertainment - a valuable and valued form of leisure-time activity which they can choose to do or not to do.

Of course, what and how much children watch needs to be controlled to some extent by parents; but the sooner children are encouraged to make choices and discriminations for themselves, the better it will be for them in the long run, even though their choices may often seem quite inexplicable to grown up tastes.

Maire Messenger Davies *Television is Good for Your Kids*

Screened Off From The Joys Of Literature

In Ray Bradbury's fantasy of the future, Fahrenheit 451, a passive population watches wall-to-wall television while firemen burn books – all literature is subversive and banned by the government. His version should touch a tender nerve in parents. Two-thirds of British children's week-day leisure time is spent watching television – roughly three hours a day. This weekly average of 23 hours is twice as much as their parents spent in front of the box as children 30 years ago, albeit a trifle less than the 29 hours the average adult now watches each week.

Susan Prest, who teaches North Oxford juniors is pessimistic about the effect of television on children's literacy. "In the last 20 years I've witnessed a very marked downward spiral in the length of time children spend reading, and also in the length of the books they choose to read. The nine-year-olds are less and less literate, they're also much less adventurous readers, and I'm sure that's because it's infinitely easier to flop in front of the television than to get into a worthwhile book."

Does it really matter that children are getting their culture through a screen instead of the written word? I think it does. In the long run, after all, reading means independence of thought. There aren't many educational tasks left to parents these days, but instilling a habit of reading is among the most important. We need to pull out the plug of the TV, take children to bookshops and libraries, encourage them to be critical about what they find there, and lobby to keep up the standards that exist.

Christina Hardyment from *The Independent*

Research The Critics Overlook

There is a pervading, largely middle-class parental view that television is bad for children. The violence shown in popular television series is believed to play a significant part in encouraging children to adopt aggressive tendencies which contribute to delinquency.

Television is also attacked for being intellectually limiting. Viewing is seen as a passive "activity" and that passivity as extending to other areas of a child's life. It is said to discourage children from reading, learning to play instruments, or talking among themselves. But have the critics been fair?

TV watching does not inevitably turn children into zombies. And just because they enjoy watching television, it does not automatically follow they do not spend time on other things as well. Research by the Independent Broadcasting Authority (IBA) has found no evidence to support the view that the availability and use of television *per se* reduces children's reading.

If television impedes other activities, then removing TV ought to produce significant changes in behaviour. Television deprivation studies from Australia, Iceland and Sweden show that this is not the case: in the absence of TV, those who read or went out the most were those who already did so.

Australian research among children aged six to twelve shows that children themselves identify TV with learning about social customs, events in the outside world, other people, and dealing with parents. Children don't simply watch impassively. A considered look at how they use TV shows that it is a far more varied and complex process than is often assumed.

Barrie Gunter *The Guardian*

Looking at both sides

1 Take each article in turn and list the main arguments being made for and against the influence of television.

2 Using these notes as your starting point, write an essay which presents and considers the arguments from both sides of the television debate, before drawing your own conclusions.

You will need to organise your material as well as your thoughts clearly before you begin to write.

One possible essay structure would be:

a general introduction – explaining why watching television is such a controversial issue

arguments against watching television – based on the information presented here as well as your own experience, but using your own words

arguments in favour of watching television – use a similar structure to the arguments against

summary of key points – bring together what you consider to be the strongest arguments on both sides

your own personal conclusion – you could come down strongly on one side or the other or you may not be able to decide. State your position clearly and indicate your reasons for holding this view.

HELP

For more help on note making and preparing to write, see the **Heinemann English Assessment and Reference File** pages 70 to 73 and 78 to 79.

Arguing for a point of view

Instead of presenting both sides of the argument you could argue strongly for one point of view, setting out to persuade people that your view is the right one.

For example, British Action for Children's Television – BAC TV is a national organisation which believes that television can be a great asset in children's lives when used well.

BAC TV campaigns for *variety* – a wide range of children's programmes across the week, information as well as entertainment.

BAC TV campaigns for *quality* – original, well-made programmes which are often costly to make. A drama series such as Grange Hill is much more expensive than an imported toy-based series like Thundercats or Ninja Turtles.

Working as individuals or in pairs, design, write and produce an effective publicity leaflet for BAC TV which aims to convince parents and teachers that television can be a good thing for children.

(Do not use more than two full sides of A4 or four, fold-over pages of A5.)
Think about:
- what you want to say – which issues are most important for you, and your audience of parents and teachers?
- how you want to say it – how best can you convince your target audience of the strength of your case?
- the way your leaflet should look – how can it both attract and hold attention?

Use a desktop publishing programme if you can – but a lot can be achieved with plain paper, a biro and a few felt-tips!

HEINEMANN ENGLISH 4 TEACHER'S PACK
You will find photocopiable sheets giving arguments for and against television in the **Teacher's Pack**.

MORE THAN JUST
POCKET MONEY

This unit asks you to discuss and write about the good and the bad points of part-time employment.

The Law in Great Britain

This is a summary of the main points of the national legislation for those under 16 years of age. Local authorities each have their own bye-laws in addition to these.

1   You may not work until the age of 13.
2   You may not work during school hours.
3   You may not work before 7.00 am or after 7.00 pm.
4   You may not work for more than 2 hours on a school day.
5   You may not work more than 5 hours per day until you are 15.
6   You may not work more than 25 hours per week until you are 15.
7   You may not work for more than 4 hours without a break.
8   You may not work for more than 2 hours on a Sunday.
9   You may work on Sunday only between 7.00 am and 11.00 am.
10 You may not do kitchen work.
11 You may not work in clubs and pubs.
12 You may not operate dangerous machines.
13 You may not clean windows which are above 3 metres high.
14 You may not do heavy or dangerous farm work.
15 You may not collect rags or refuse.
16 You may not work in a slaughter house.
17 You may not work at a racecourse.
18 You may not deliver fuel oils.
19 You may not work without your parent's permission.
20 You may not work without your headteacher's permission.

Debating the Law

- What do you think of the Law?
- For how many of the rules can you see a good reason?
- Which rules seem out-of-date or unnecessary?
- Which two rules would you make the greatest effort to enforce if you were the police?
- Which two rules would you be keenest to see changed?
- Many people have said that the law on part-time employment for people under 16 needs to be simplified. Try to draw up a simple code on part-time employment that would be sensible, fair and enforceable.

NO SLAVE LABOUR

What actually happens

Discovering what happens in real life as opposed to what should happen can be difficult. Read the following statements:

1 Four out of ten children between the ages of 12 and 16 at any one time have a part-time job.
2 Three-quarters of those who have a part-time job are working illegally.
3 Many are able to get part-time jobs before the age of 13.
4 Many work illegal hours.
5 Many jobs involve heavy lifting.
6 Many do not have work permits.
7 Many are quite happy to work illegally.
8 Many feel exploited but need the money.
9 In many cases, the employer is a parent, relative or friend.
10 One in three have been injured in some way at work.

Debating what happens

- How many of the statements about what actually happens agree with your experience? Give evidence to support your views.
- How many of the statements are not supported by your experience? Again, give evidence to support your views.
- Decide on three statements that sum up the most important aspects of part-time working for you. It would be best if you came up with your own statements but you may choose statements from the list.

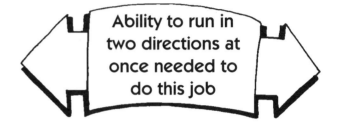

Investigating the subject

Write a report on one of the following aspect of part-time work based on your own research:

1 **Attitudes to part-time work**
   Collect opinions from a variety of sources, for example; parents, teachers, employers, young people under 16 with or without jobs.

2 **The Law**
   Use the information in this unit to write a quiz/ questionnaire about the law on part-time working and test the knowledge of different people. For example, do adults know more about the law than young people or vice versa?

3 **Conditions of work**
   Conduct a survey into what it is like to have a part-time job. Amongst the areas you could look at are:
   - rates of pay
   - hours of work
   - type of work
   - behaviour of bosses towards part-time staff.

4 **Case studies**
   You could look at two or three people's jobs in detail, for example:
   - compare the part-time jobs of a parent and a member of your class
   - compare three people who each do a morning newspaper round but for different shops.

Should young people be encouraged to take up part-time jobs?

What do you think?

Write an essay that considers whether part-time jobs are a good or a bad thing for young people. Direct your work at a teacher who has little experience in this area and wants to be better informed.

Start by making a list of reasons for and against having a part-time job. Use the discussions you have had, the investigations you have made and the information you have been given to help you. The opinions expressed below may give you some further ideas.

Should young people be encouraged to take up part time jobs?	
FOR	AGAINST
freedom of choice – if adults can why not us? getting money to enjoy what leisure time is available after working.	exploitation –find out how much friends are paid exam results can suffer – look at time required to do homework well.

I use young people because I don't have to pay them very much. If I don't like them, I can sack them and there's no come-back.

See this? It took three years' work but it's been worth every second. And I've learnt tons of things they never teach you in school.

Dad's been out of work for five years. Everyone in our house is expected to do something.

My two daughters help me because one day this will all be theirs. They don't earn very much as yet because they aren't worth very much as yet...but they will be and they will appreciate the training they were given.

Three of my friends are hardly ever in school these days because their part-time jobs have become almost full-time. They may not be losing out yet but they will when it comes to exams and qualifications. They're stupid really.

CREATIVE WRITING

People who never have to write a story sometimes think it is the easiest thing in the world. It isn't. If you have ever been given a free choice of title for your writing, you will know how difficult it can be to come up with a good idea. The aim of this section is to give you some guidelines to follow.

Can I use personal experience?

Yes, but you do not have to tell a story exactly as it happened, you can use what happened as a basis for your writing. The great advantage in basing something on personal experience is that you know how it feels and so your writing is more likely to be believable.

Can I imagine anything?

Yes, but some things may work better than others. For example, horror and thriller writing are more difficult to do well than fantasy or science fiction. It is not enough to copy Stephen King, for example, if you want to write a horror story. Your version will be disappointing by comparison. If you are going to write in a particular style or genre you need to be doing something that makes your writing stand out. It has to be **yours** and not just a copy of someone else's work. Imaginative writing is not separate from personal writing either. Some of the best horror stories have been based on an unpleasant experience suffered by the writer. If you can make your reader believe in what is happening, even if it is on a planet that is 2000 light years from here, then you are more than half way to success. Remember that, even in a distant galaxy, your characters have to seem real.

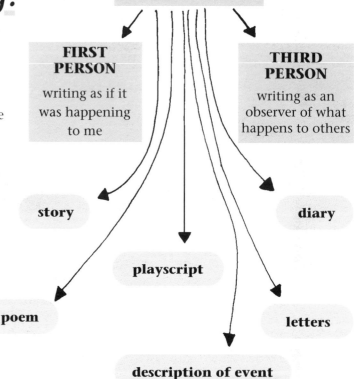

What form can I use?

FIRST PERSON

writing as if it was happening to me

THIRD PERSON

writing as an observer of what happens to others

story

diary

playscript

poem

letters

description of event

What if I don't know where to start?

Sometimes the right title can give you an idea. Take a look at these and use them or make up your own. Ask a friend what they would choose. Ask them to suggest further titles.

Another rotten valentine
Second chance
Their holiday, not mine
Fatty
I never touched it
The promise

Absolute beginners
No one's going to change my life
Getting away with it
Time to leave
Bully
Just try it once

And, if I'm still stuck...?

Look at the photographs that illustrate this section. What might have happened in the time before the photograph was taken?

What might happen in the next few minutes/hours/days/weeks?

Write down as quickly as possible any thoughts that occur to you and don't worry about sorting them out until later. Ideas have a bad habit of disappearing if they do not get fixed on paper.

The real problem is getting started

That's exactly what people who write for their living say as well. Sometimes being given an opening sentence or two helps. The simple act of writing down a few words that someone else has written gets the brain going. Here are several openings including some which might work for the photographs in this section:

I had always thought that our home was the one place where I was safe...

He was the sort of person who would try almost anything to make money...

We shouldn't have been climbing all over it. In fact, we shouldn't have been anywhere near it...

When the tragedy happened, you knew, in minutes, who your real friends were...

From the weight of the hand on my shoulder, I knew it was the store detective...

"You can't keep that thing in the house," cried...

The only thing that stopped me becoming permanently rigid with boredom was the faint hope that...

"How long have you been up there?" asked...

I had never won anything in my life...

She told them she was sorry. She would have cried to prove it to them if she could but it had gone beyond tears...

He just didn't look as if he would be interesting to talk to so most people politely ignored him for the first half term...

"Don't try to do it all by yourself," they had said. Did I listen? No...

And, if nothing inspires me...?

You don't have to be inspired to start writing, you just have to have an idea, a situation, a group of people or an incident that suggests a beginning to you. Try it like this.

- Write down as many actual people as you can think of who might appear in a story of yours. *Not just your friends, people like the headteacher or the welfare officer as well.*
- Then write down as many situations as you can think of in which they might appear.
- Then decide whether you want to appear in your own story.
- Finally decide which situation will be the opening for your writing.

Suggest some situations...

Saturday night in town

The day after some vandalism at the school

Two boys interested in one girl (or vice versa)

Non-attendance at school

An anorexic friend needs help

The local park one evening

Problems with the boss at your Saturday job

Difficulties with parents

My pencil case is another planet (– well, it's different!)

You can also find a series of situations that could be used on pages 58 and 59 in the unit *Honest I would.*

I'll never come up with anything

Yes, you will. Everyone can tell stories. Just put people in a good mood and the stories start to flow. If you are really still stuck and are not just moaning, then try listening to people and re-telling one of the stories you hear over the next few days. Ask your friends what stories they would tell about you. And don't give them a black eye for their answer – write it down.

WARNING: DISASTER AHEAD

Avoid these!

1 Too many characters
2 Too much dialogue in a story
3 "Borrowing" ideas from television or video
4 Well-used endings such as "and then I woke up"

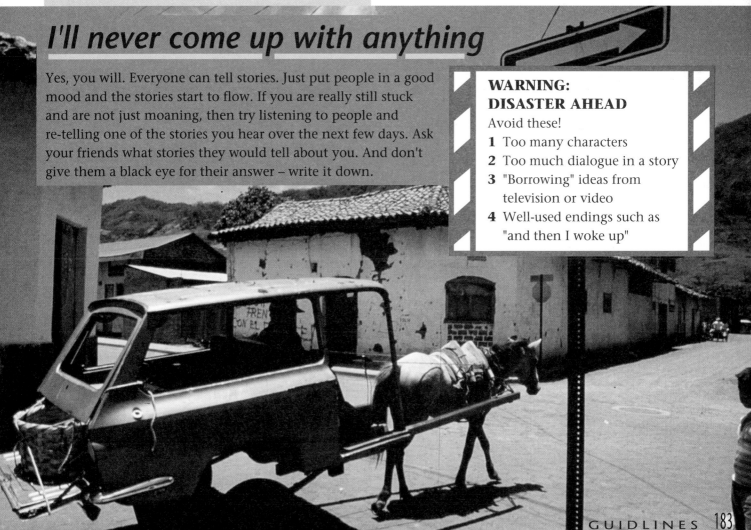

WRITING TO INFORM OR PERSUADE

You may sometimes be asked to write on any subject about which you feel strongly. You could also be asked to write an informative piece about any subject which you know well. This section will help you decide what to write about and how to write it.

Can I choose any subject?

If you have been given a free choice the answer is *yes* as long as it is not likely to cause offence. On the other hand, some subjects work better than others. If you are being tested on your ability to organise information, you have got to have the information in the first place. If you are being asked to express an opinion, it is pretty silly to choose a subject about which you have no views whatsoever.

So I'm fine as long as I've got loads of material?

Not quite. Material needs to be organised. The information you can find in books needs to be re-shaped into your own way of writing.

The information also needs to be related to your own knowledge and experience. This is best explained by an example. Two students in one group a few years ago chose dogs as a subject for their writing. Both worked very hard. Both used the library and visited the local vet's surgery for leaflets. One of them wrote up what she had found. The other one used what she had found but also wrote about the experience gained in owning two dogs and working at the kennels during the previous summer. It was the second writer who achieved the high mark because she made good use of her experience. If you can follow her example, you will be giving yourself the best chance of a good grade. Experience does not always have to be something that has happened to you, it can also be something you have seen happen to those around you. For example, you do not have to be bullied to know something about bullying!

> **WARNING**
> You are not showing your ability to use information by copying it all out in your best handwriting or putting it on your wordprocessor. It is not much better to take sentences from a book or a leaflet and change a word or two.

How do I begin?

All writers need to know for whom they are writing. Sometimes this is clearer than others. If you write a letter to a friend you know exactly who your audience is. If you write for a magazine you have an idea of who is likely to read that particular magazine but you cannot be as certain as you could be with the letter. Even if you are writing a fairly general essay it will help to be specific about your audience. For example, are you writing for a teacher, for adults in general, for students in your own year group or for whom? In the section *Words to communicate* there are plenty of examples of pieces of writing with specific audiences. In most cases, this makes the writing easier because it is clearer what you are doing. Look at pages 114-117 and 119 to see how this works out in practice.

What kind of writing am I doing?

That's a good question. It is mainly a matter of deciding how best to communicate with your audience. Here are some of the most common ways of reaching your audience:

magazine or newspaper article   essay
letters   leaflet

If you are trying to give a subject maximum publicity, you may decide to use a variety of means. If you were campaigning for the abolition of school uniform, for example, you might write letters to teachers, parents and the local newspaper. In addition, you might produce posters and a leaflet for use in school.

TWO HINTS

1 Posters and other beautiful artwork are not a good excuse for failing to write more than a handful of words. You will be judged in the end on your use of the English language.

2 Many people opt to write newspaper reports even though they hardly ever pick up a newspaper. Journalism is an underrated and difficult skill. If you rarely read newspapers or have little confidence in this area, leave it alone.

What about organising it all?

NOTE MAKING
If you find making notes difficult, you will find it useful to look at the unit *Sorting it out* on page 137.

1 Be clear where you are starting from
Make brief notes about what you already know of the subject.
Decide what you think you need to find out.

2 Do your research
Remember that the reference sections of libraries are stuffed full of facts, but opinions and experiences are often best discovered from people. Most pieces of writing will tend to require both fact and opinion. There is a temptation as a writer to present a lot of facts because they are easier to deal with. Remember that, for the reader, the more interesting parts will be those that relate people's experiences and their opinions.

3 Plan your writing
This is easier to say than to do. Some people choose their opening point, their finishing point and give everything else in between a number. Some people look for evidence for and against an idea and put everything in one of two columns, which can obviously work well when you are considering two sides of an argument. Other people start by drawing a diagram to show how all the sections and ideas might link up. The diagrams over the page illustrate two of these approaches.

chances to learn in a real job

People's rights to choose what they do with their life

NO

Should school leaving age be raised to 18 years?

YES

You cannot get a decent job without proper training

People will be reluctant to train unless everyone is doing it

Should people smoke?

FOR	AGAINST
other people do	health dangers to yourself
relaxation	health dangers to others
looking more adult	smelling like a chimney

4 Write your first draft

You need all the material you are going to use within arm's reach. Many people find that they get the best results if they can write the first draft in one sitting. That is not always possible but it is worth a try. Open by making it clear what you will say and how you will say it and end by summing up what you have said.

5 Edit your material

Go through your first draft, pruning, replacing and reorganising material. If any of it is waffle, cut it. If anything repeats what you have already said, think seriously about whether you need it.

6 Proof read the material

You need to check spelling, punctuation and paragraphing. Remember that speech is easiest to read when a new speaker is given a new line. To avoid very long paragraphs, you may need to break some of your arguments into two or three parts. Keep a careful watch as well to check that you haven't run two or three sentences together.

7 Re-draft the material

You know what you mean but will other people? Are there parts that could be made clearer? Are there points that require an illustration or an example? Could a particular point be made more simply and hence more effectively? Many writers will re-draft at the same time as they proof read but it is certainly worth reading through at least once more after the proof reading stage to check that everything is crystal clear.

Suggest some subjects

The best we can do is tell you some of the subjects which other students have tackled successfully. Remember that it is how you approach the subject that matters most and not just the subject. Here is the list:

A guide to the school for newcomers

A survival guide for new teachers

Smoking: information for the tempted
a leaflet on kicking the habit

Abortion: right or wrong?

Coping with parents: a series of advice letters to a friend

Equal opportunities: a study of race, sex, handicap or all three

Experiments on animals: can they ever be justified?

Meat or just vegetables: the great food debate

Nuclear power: cheap energy or expensive suicide?

Leaving school at 14: an argument for new kinds of education

And if I'm still stuck?

Listen to yourself outside the classroom. Everyone has opinions about certain things and most people are happy to become involved in an argument or two. Once you have discovered what you speak up about, bring that subject back into the English lesson and start shaping it into written form.

> **FURTHER HELP**
> In **Heinemann English Assessment and Reference File**, there are information sheets on note making, pages 70 to 73, letter writing, pages 74 to 77, news reporting, pages 80 to 81, making a leaflet, pages 82 to 83 and redrafting, page 86.

WIDER READING

If you enjoy a good read, being asked to choose a book to write about is no great problem. If you hate the very sight of a library or a bookshop, you have a problem. Whether you love or hate books, the experience of other students can help you choose ones you are likely to enjoy.

If you are an active reader...

...you will probably have very clear views about the kind of books you enjoy. Take the opportunity to extend your interests. This does not mean dropping romantic fiction for war books or moving from fantasy to Russian novelists! If you enjoy modern fantasy, look at George Orwell's *Animal Farm* which mixes politics and imagination in a different way to current writers. If you have read several Agatha Christie novels, you might try P D James or Ruth Rendell. Talk to other readers and find out what they have enjoyed.

If you only read when you have to...

... you will need to find a book that grabs your attention in the first few pages and has plenty in it to keep you reading. This is not as impossible as it sounds and the *Writers to explore* list is a good place to start. *Twenty Further Titles* provide some extra ideas. The lists are not just a teacher's choice, they also include the books that a range of 14 to 16 year old readers have enjoyed. Those consulted included students who only read if there was a teacher behind them and a deadline in front of them.

Writers to explore

Janni Howker   There is something about the way that Janni Howker writes that makes you believe that what you are reading is actually happening. In *The Nature of the Beast* that can be very disturbing. The book is not a horror story although the 'beast' turns out to be all too real. Other books include *Isaac Campion* and a collection of short stories called *Badger on the Barge*.

James Watson   Here is another very believable writer, perhaps because he once worked as a journalist. His novel *Talking in Whispers* is set in Chile and tells the story of Andres not only as his father is assassinated but more especially as he himself comes to know too much. The book is chilling when you remember that it is based on what has already happened to many people in that country. Other books include *Freedom Tree, Where Nobody Sees* and *Make Your Move* from which the story on page 6 comes.

Robert Swindells   His book about life after the bomb, *Brother in the Land*, is recommended not only because it is disturbingly believable but because the situation is constantly changing, which means that you keep reading to see how it works out. The main character, Danny, is described as one of the unlucky ones because he survived the initial bomb blast. If you read to the end, you will know why. Other books by Robert Swindells include *Voyage to Valhalla, Room 13* and *The Serpent's Tooth*.

Joan Lingard   Although most of her life has been lived in Scotland, her early years were spent in Northern Ireland. Her most popular novel *Across the Barricades* describes what happens when Sadie, a Protestant girl, and Kevin, a Catholic boy, start to become much more than friends. If you enjoy books about people's lives then this may be for you. The books that continue Sadie and Kevin's story are *Into Exile, A Proper Place* and *Hostages to Fortune*.

Nigel Hinton   A writer who is best known for *Buddy*, the story of a boy who would like to have similar parents to everyone else but learns painfully how to cope with the ones he has got. Other books include *Buddy's Song* and *Getting Free*.

Paul Zindel   He made his name with *The Pigman*, an unusual story of two young people who befriend an old man and unwittingly cause his death. His novels often mix zany humour and sad realities. They include *The Pigman's Legacy, Pardon me, You're Stepping on My Eyeball, I Never Loved Your Mind* and *A Begonia for Miss Applebaum*.

Robert Westall   Best known for his war-time novel *The Machine Gunners*, this writer is also fascinated by the paranormal. Look out for *Break of Dark, The Scarecrows, Blitz Cat, Fathom Five, Kingdom by the Sea* and *Urn Burial*.

Roald Dahl   A man who often infuriated adults who are rarely pictured sympathetically in his books. His adult fiction is less popular than his books for children but his two - part autobiography *Boy* and *Going Solo* is an entertaining and enjoyable read. There are also his short - story collections.

Pam Conrad   A writer with a very readable style. In *Holding me Here*, Robin's curiosity about the family's new lodger gets the better of her. Afterwards, she often wishes that it hadn't. Other books include *A Seal Upon my Hear*t and *Taking the Ferry Home*.

Ray Bradbury   For many people, he is still the master of the science fiction short story. One of the most popular collections is *The Golden Apples of the Sun* but look out as well for *The Illustrated Man, The October Country* and *The Silver Locusts*. Bradbury is also unusual in that you do not need to be a science fiction fan to enjoy his stories.

Rosa Guy   Life is never easy for the young people in Rosa Guy's novels. Take Imamu in *The Disappearance*. He has spent only two days with his new foster parents when their small daughter disappears and he becomes number one suspect. Take a look at *The Friends, Ruby* and *Edith Jackson* as well.

Twenty further titles

1 *Does this school have capital punishment?* - Nat Hentoff
2 *Z for Zachariah* – Robert C O'Brien
3 *The Diary of a teenage health freak* – Aidan Macfarlane/Ann McPherson
4 *Fat* - Barbara Wersba
5 *Locked in Time* – Lois Duncan
6 *The Changeover* – Margaret Mahy
7 *Words by Heart* – Ouida Sebestyen
8 *Eight plus One* – Robert Cormier
9 *Children of the Dust* – Louise Lawrence
10 *Salt on the Snow* – Rukshana Smith
11 *It's my life* – Robert Leeson
12 *A Proper Little Nooryeff* – Jean Ure
13 *Granny was a Buffer Girl* – Berlie Doherty
14 *The Fox in Winter* – John Branfield
15 *Andi's War* – Billi Rosen
16 *Zak* – Frances Thomas
17 *The Outsiders* – S E Hinton
18 *Troublemaker* – Rex Harley
19 *Waiting for the Rain* – Sheila Gordon
20 *Snapshots of Paradise* – Adèle Geras

How do I write about a book?

If you have chosen a book with which your teachers are familiar, they will have several ideas for your writing. Where a book is less well known, they may suggest a more general assignment such as one of these:

1 The Review

The most important thing you can do for a book you have enjoyed is to encourage someone else to read it. This is basically what reviewing is all about: telling other people what something is like so they can share it. (If it is poor, you tell them so they can avoid it.) A good reviewer will:

- give title and author so that a reader can follow up the review
- give a general idea of what the book is about
- write about some of the book's characters, themes and incidents
- give a personal response
- make clear to whom the book might appeal
- make sure the ending is not given away.

2 The diary of a main character

If you feel there is a character in the book that you understand well, you could show that by writing his or her diary for some of the important events covered by the book. A diary will include not only what happened but how people felt about what happened. Diary writing is the subject of the unit *Punished for your language* on page 30.

3 A character remembers

This is a version of the previous idea. Instead of using the diary format, imagine that one of the characters wants to talk about or write down their account of some of the important events covered by the book. Deciding what would be important to this character is crucial to doing this successfully.

4 An additional chapter

Another way to show that you understand the characters in a book and their relationship to each other is to write an extra chapter or scene in which they appear. The key to doing this successfully is the ability to write in the style of the book and make the characters behave consistently.

5 Dramatisation

Turning a part of the book into drama or into filmscript is a fascinating challenge because it gives you the opportunity to think about how the story could be brought to life in a different format. It is much better to dramatise a small part of the book well than to do a large chunk adequately. You can look at the potential for dramatisation by turning to the unit *The Story of an Hour* on page 90.

6 Comparison

A good way to get your own thinking about a book clearer is to contrast it with another. You could choose to compare two books by the same writer or the way that two books treat the same theme.

7 Study guide

One way of showing a wide and detailed understanding of a single book is to produce a study guide for it that could be used by other students of your age. Choose a layout that will help make your material clear and easily understood. Subjects that you will normally need to cover are:

- plot
- characters
- themes
- style
- overall effect.

This is the most difficult of the choices but it gives you the chance to show the greatest range of skills.

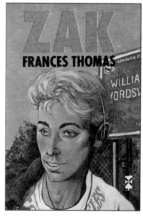

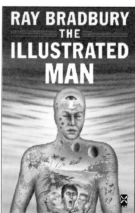

FURTHER HELP

Heinemann English Assessment and Reference File contains information sheets on reading logs, page 87, film and television scripts, pages 97 to 99 and playscripts, page 100.

WHERE TO FIND IT

This index does not try to indicate every place where you can look at a subject or practise a skill. However, it does highlight the units where these subjects are mainly dealt with. Some units are given under more than one heading.

FURTHER HELP
The **Heinemann English Assessment and Reference File** includes information sheets on most aspects of using English that are not covered here, from finding your way around a library to putting commas in the right places.